P9-CEA-360

More Praise for *The Art of Convening*

"Patricia and Craig's book will bring a deeper level of joy and meaning into your conversations, your gatherings, and your life."

—Dr. Mark Albion, author of *Making a Life, Making a Living* and former Harvard Business School professor

"As a longtime 'meeting hater,' I found the Neals' book a mind-opener."

—Peter Barnes, cofounder, Working Assets, and author of *Capitalism 3.0*

"Simple and yet profound. A book that gets to the heart of what it means to be an authentic leader."

—Richard Barrett, author of *Building a Values-Driven Organization*

"This book is a clear way forward for leaders—not only to great meetings but into solid relationships, big solutions, and meaningful work."

—Elizabeth Becker, President and CEO, Professional BusinessWomen of California

"This book is timely, practical, and filled with wisdom."

—Alan Briskin, coauthor of *The Power of Collective Wisdom*

"Incorporate the principles and practices of this book knowing happiness is a measurable indicator of smart business and good living."

—Chip Conley, Executive Chairman and Chief Creative Officer, Joie de Vivre

"This book offers us an indispensable tool, like a flashlight or Swiss Army knife on a camping trip, to take everywhere."

—Aryae Coopersmith, founder and CEO, HR Forums

"An inspiring and practical book to show us the way."

—Bruce Cryer, CEO, HeartMath

"An elegant, practical guide on how to create and hold space for people in a manner that ignites deep engagement and exploration."

—Mary Jo Kreitzer PhD, founder and Director, Center for Spirituality and Healing, University of Minnesota

"If you want to learn how to lead successful gatherings, skim *The Art of Convening*. If you want to learn how to lead *transformational* gatherings, read it from cover to cover."

—Deb Nelson, Executive Director, Social Venture Network

"Turn 'meetings' of the sort we complain about into the live and engaging encounters that real living requires."

—Parker J. Palmer, author of *A Hidden Wholeness* and *Let Your Life Speak*

"The Neals bring groups, even contentious ones, to deep truths and positive commitment in relatively short times."

—Michael Ray, Professor of Creativity and Innovation, Emeritus, Stanford Graduate School of Business, and author of *The Highest Goal*

"The nuggets of wisdom will stay with you for a long time as you practice its art form in creating meaningful and profound conversations."

—Ann Schrader, Chief Operating Officer, HealthEast Care System

"This book is a trustworthy guide for anyone who wishes to serve powerful gatherings and the emergence of true community."

—David Sibbet, founder, The Grove Consultants International, and author of *Visual Meetings*

"The clear, articulation of the 'technology of relationships' in this book opens the door for authentic engagement in any encounter."

—Lynne Twist, author of *The Soul of Money* and President, Soul of Money Institute

"The authors have done for convening what Julia Child did for the art of French cooking—they have created the definitive and authoritative guide for *mastering* the art of convening. *Bon appétit!*"

—Eric Utne, founder, *Utne Reader*

"*The Art of Convening* outlines, in detail, the principles and practical application of convening we used on our road to success."

—David Wagner, Owner and Daymaker, Juut Salonspa, and author of *Life as a Daymaker*

"Seldom have I encountered such depth of wisdom and clarity of process presented with such a gentle, inviting spirit."

—Margaret J. Wheatley, author of *Leadership and the New Science*

Full versions of these endorsements and additional endorsements can be found at http://heartlandcircle.com/aocendorsements.htm.

THE ART OF CONVENING

THE ART OF CONVENING

AUTHENTIC ENGAGEMENT IN MEETINGS, GATHERINGS, AND CONVERSATIONS

By **CRAIG** and **PATRICIA NEAL**

with **CYNTHIA WOLD**

Berrett–Koehler Publishers, Inc.
San Francisco
a BK Business book

Berrett-Koehler Publishers, Inc.
235 Montgomery Street, Suite 650
San Francisco, CA 94104-2916
Tel: (415) 288-0260 Fax: (415) 362-2512 www.bkconnection.com

Ordering Information
Quantity sales. Special discounts are available on quantity purchases by corporations, associations, and others. For details, contact the "Special Sales Department" at the Berrett-Koehler address above.
Individual sales. Berrett-Koehler publications are available through most bookstores. They can also be ordered directly from Berrett-Koehler: Tel: (800) 929-2929; Fax: (802) 864-7626; www.bkconnection.com
Orders for college textbook/course adoption use. Please contact Berrett-Koehler: Tel: (800) 929-2929; Fax: (802) 864-7626.
Orders by U.S. trade bookstores and wholesalers. Please contact Ingram Publisher Services, Tel: (800) 509-4887; Fax: (800) 838-1149; E-mail: customer.service@ingrampublisherservices.com; or visit www.ingrampublisherservices.com/Ordering for details about electronic ordering.

Printed in the United States of America
Berrett-Koehler books are printed on long-lasting acid-free paper. When it is available, we choose paper that has been manufactured by environmentally responsible processes. These may include using trees grown in sustainable forests, incorporating recycled paper, minimizing chlorine in bleaching, or recycling the energy produced at the paper mill.

Library of Congress Cataloging-in-Publication Data
Neal, Craig.
The art of convening : authentic engagement in meetings, gatherings and conversations / by Craig and Patricia Neal, with Cynthia Wold. — 1st ed.
p. cm.
Includes bibliographical references and index.
ISBN 978-1-60509-668-1 (pbk.)
1. Business meetings. 2. Meetings. 3. Communication in organizations. 4. Group facilitation. I. Neal, Patricia, 1953– II. Wold, Cynthia. III. Title.
HF5734.5.N43 2011
658.4'56—dc22 2010029459

First Edition
16 15 14 13 12 11 10 9 8 7 6 5 4 3 2

Interior design & illustration: Laura Lind Design
Proofreader: Henrietta Bensussen
Book producer: Linda Jupiter Productions
Cover design: Irene Morris
Copyeditor: Elissa Rabellino
Indexer: J. Naomi Linzer

This book is dedicated to the people of the

Thought Leader Gathering, Art of Convening Training,

and Heartland communities,

whose loving support has sustained the

evolution of this book.

CONTENTS

FOREWORD

Called to Convene

Writing this foreword has been a rare and special privilege. I've spent many hours with Craig and Patricia Neal, since they live in my home city of Minneapolis. I have experienced their call to convene. They bring to that calling and to the community here a very special presence. They show us how to be completely human while at the same time understanding the complex and fragile enterprise of convening work. For their courage and their willingness to be transparent companions and guides to their colleagues near and far, we are grateful.

The Heartland authors invite us into the circle that is their calling. They take us into their heart lands where the spirit of convening resides and where we connect with our inner wisdom. They gently prod us to exit the fast lane and move into the slow lane of purpose and practice, which summons us to heed our own call to convene. Many of us are called to convening work by a sense that we can make a difference in someone's life, in our world.

Convening was, and is, one of the most powerful, life-altering forces in the universe. The genesis of this book can be traced back to the art of convening to energize communities and stir us to survive and envision what might be possible. The modern practice of convening has ancient roots. There was a time when spirit, work, and life were integrated. Early peoples hunted, gathered, cooked, and naturally convened. The poet T. S. Eliot described those roots precisely when he asked in his poem "The Rock,"

Where is the wisdom we have lost in knowledge?

Where is the knowledge we have lost in information?

This book recovers that lost wisdom we are yearning for today.

On its surface, the book shares pioneering practices on "how to" be a successful convener. But that is not the core gift of the book. The book is distinct and valuable because it is a clear expression of the integrity and spirit of its authors. This gift of consistently ensuring that words and practices are of one spirit is just what is too often missing in the convening process itself.

Heeding the call to convene requires a clear choice—the choice to be authentically ourselves. Each convener is an experiment of one. Our calling is like our signature, footprint, or thumbprint—uniquely ours. Being authentically engaged means that we realize we are here to contribute to life on earth something that no one else can contribute in quite the same way.

One golden thread woven into the fabric of this book is the embrace of the spiritual essence of our lives. Many organizations are a reflection of the rational mind. They operate on strictly rational models as a basis for leadership and behavior. It is often this exclusive belief that gets in the way of the very transformation or engagement they are seeking.

Organizations are human communities, driven as much by emotions and spirit as by reason. Spirit is the energy fundamental to authentic engagement. It is the animating or activating force in great convening work. When we are in touch with spirit, we feel whole and alive. If we split spirit out of our lives or deny it in our work or community, we feel a sense of deadness. This book restores wholeness—it brings aliveness back to life, work, and community.

Many, many books come across my reading table each year, but it has been a long time since one of them affected me as much as this one has. It has struck some deep chords within me. It has reminded me that each gathering is a sacred adventure where even our struggles can lead us to what mythologist Joseph Campbell called "the rapture of being alive." You hold in your hands a wise book. I hope it brings you alive like it did me.

—*Richard J. Leider*

Author of The Power of Purpose: Find Meaning, Live Longer, Better *and coauthor of* Repacking Your Bags: Lighten Your Load for the Rest of Your Life

WELCOME

Bringing authentic engagement to meetings, gatherings, and conversations is an essential leadership skill that improves outcomes and brings connection and positive transformation to our companies, organizations, clubs, communities, families, and friendships.

Welcome to the world of *convening*: the art of gathering and "holding" people for the sake of authentic engagement.

Much of the focus of the Art of Convening, the practice we developed for holding authentic meetings, is about preparing ourselves internally for a gathering, which leads to how we interact with others in our gatherings, and how we observe and shepherd the interactions of participants with each other. Why does this matter?

Most of us really want to be effective and truly engaged with others. We go into meetings or gatherings with high expectations for good outcomes. We decide to do something—together. We want to make a plan, come to a real consensus, innovate, or pool our energies. Sometimes we may just wish to know each other better or celebrate a milestone together.

What we often hear about this feature of life that most of us experience as a necessity in our careers, families, and friendships is

> "Meetings are a waste of time."
>
> "These gatherings are boring."

"People don't mean what they say."

"Phone conferences are useless."

"The same people always talk."

"Am I really needed?"

It is unfortunate that we react this way to meetings that have come to dominate the workday, whether virtual or in person, and that we sometimes dread gatherings where families, colleagues, or friends may endure each other with smiles and chatter while impatiently watching the clock for the proper time to exit.

Why do we so often perceive meetings as a waste of time? Why are gatherings boring? Why do our conversations fall flat? To bring the kind of meaning and outcome that most of us yearn for when we gather, the key quality needed is *authentic engagement.*

Authentic engagement with another, or others, is not tiring or draining. It is not one-sided, manipulating, persuading, or controlling. Authentic engagement is, simply, a genuine expression of what is true for us, and an attentive listening to what is true for another, or others. Why this simple human interaction often eludes us can be a matter of habit, distrust, faulty modeling, lack of attention, or fear.

This book offers a set of practices and principles that will lead to authentic engagement and authentic leadership in our meetings, our gatherings, and our conversations (one-on-one or more). These practices and principles are at the nexus of leadership development and personal development, and will bring an integrated, whole-systems dimension to those who use them.

We have experienced and observed, in our own work and lives, the power of authentic engagement to bring a shift of energy to a meeting or gathering. When authentically engaged, people tend to feel energized and connected, which leads to better outcomes. This shift in energy often generates meaningful conversation, an emergence of something new, and an alignment that leads to true commitment from those who participate.

The Convening Wheel model (see the introduction) helps to bring the practices and principles needed for authentic engagement together as a whole—with a natural order and sequence that can be followed, or not.

There are many books and theories about best practices in meetings or gatherings. The Art of Convening is unique in that it can be used independently, but can also be used in conjunction with other models, methods, skills, and proficiencies we already have.

We welcome you to try the Art of Convening, beginning wherever it makes sense for you, and to discover the gift of *authentic engagement* in all of its simplicity and power.

INTRODUCTION

The role of the Convener is to gather and hold the people

IT WAS A REMARKABLE MEETING of senior-level women executives, gathering to explore the notion of convening as a leadership competency. I was the Convener, but it was clear from the onset that these women were used to running their own show. Many had grown into their leadership in results-dominated environments, driving definable goals and outcomes, where listening skills and vulnerability were not often appreciated or wanted.

As the Convener, I had done a considerable amount of preparation, internal and external—but I have to admit, I was nervous. Most of those present were not familiar with Heartland's work and had never experienced the Art of Convening—and many were cutting-edge leaders in their own right, with very defined ways of doing things. I knew I would be challenged in this practice.

After the introductions and context setting, we gathered in a large circle. I reminded myself that my intention here was to bring authentic engagement to the gathering and to set aside any other motives that could interfere with that intention. Then I asked that each woman in turn speak to an important question she was dealing with as a leader. As each spoke, their responses deepening with each voice, I was reminded of why I love to do this work.

A few common themes emerged: "How do *I* have to change to bring about the change I want to see in my organization?" "How do

I create authentic connections with my people when I rush from meeting to meeting?" "I'm tired of doing things the same old way, but don't know what else there is."

Once everyone had spoken, the majority welcomed the opportunity to take a deeper dive into their challenges. The room had become electric with energy. A window had been opened to a conversation of meaning and personal consequence. And some of the participants showed palpable discomfort.

There were many competing agendas in the room, and midway through the afternoon I lost my internal focus and lost my way, getting off-track from the agenda. At this point, a key leader left the room without comment, obviously disturbed. A flash of anxiety swept over me as my stomach tightened. Would the group be able to hold together? Would we be able to complete the day?

After years of witnessing the phenomenon of group breakdown, I knew that I had to stay present. I focused again on my intention to bring authentic engagement, and suspended my judgment of others in the room and, more important, of myself. I was back on track to complete the day's agenda. The group's comfort level gradually increased, and "ahas" and nuggets of wisdom emerged. The group seemed to feel an understanding and appreciation for being together in authentic conversation.

What many of us began to see was a vision of leadership that is enhanced by the capacity to slow down for authentic engagement, and to create authentic relationship, which is at the core of why convening with intention matters.

—Patricia Neal

In 1995, Craig and Patricia Neal founded Heartland Inc., an organization offering a different kind of service—connection. As the mission states: *Heartland convenes conversations, programs, trainings, and communities of engagement to practice the skills of the intentional leader, dedicated to creating a world that works for all.*

Heartland has created and developed, among other programs, the Thought Leader Gatherings, a membership-based community of engagement for leaders since 1998; Heartland Network, a global online social media leadership community; and a suite of the Art of Convening (AoC) Trainings offering the principles, practices, and applications of convening. This book is the first public sharing of the AoC model.

Often, *convening* is used as a synonym for facilitating gatherings and meetings. Heartland has been differentiating convening from facilitating and leading meetings since its founding. By definition, *facilitation* is "the process of making something easy or easier,"[2] whereas *convening*, for Heartland, has come to mean the art of gathering and "holding" people, in a safe and generative

> ONE WAY *to encapsulate the leadership required to create an alternative future is to consider the leader as primarily a convener—not leader as special person, but leader as a citizen, sometimes with legitimate power, willing to do those things that can initiate something new in the world. In this way, "leader" belongs right up there with cook, carpenter, artist, and landscape designer. All of us can develop this ability with a small amount of teaching and an agreement to practice—the ultimate do-it-yourself movement.*
>
> —*Peter Block*[1]

space, for the sake of authentic engagement each time we invite people together, whether virtually or in person.

After many years of hosting national conferences and meetings and convening scores of Thought Leader Gatherings, we realized that we needed to write the "recipe" for how to convene. This book examines the art and practice of gathering people for the sake of authentic engagement, which we believe produces better outcomes than could be obtained otherwise—whether for fun, profit, alignment, dispute resolution, insight, wisdom, brainstorming, or problem solving. It addresses the essential principles and practices for those called to convene and lead meetings and gatherings, as well as for those of us who don't seek to lead all the time but wish to serve in the best way possible when leadership is called for.

APPLICATIONS OF CONVENING

Although the Art of Convening was developed as a leadership model, many other applications have emerged. Once we learn how to be a Convener, we may constantly find opportunities to bring authentic engagement not only to our work lives, but also to our neighborhoods, book groups, friendships, families, and personal relationships.

MY HUSBAND PLANNED A family birthday party at our house for my 15-year-old stepson. There were eight of us at the dining room table, including the two teenage brothers, engaged in three or four simultaneous conversations—teen one-upping a prominent one. In our family, attempts to be in charge are often met with great resistance, both overt and covert, so stepping in can be risky. I wondered, though, whether my learning about being a Convener could help us have a different kind of interaction and connection.

Through dinner I thought about how I would like to be in relationship with the people at the table. I clarified my intention while planning how to ask for a change in the usual family free-for-all to a more intimate way of being together. It was important to me that my motives be pure. Was I acting out of annoyance with the teenagers, a desire to assert my authority, or something hidden or unkind that could bring about a result I didn't want? I consciously set aside any ulterior motive I could think of and focused on the intention to bring authentic engagement to the group. That was all.

I finally asked everyone if it would be OK if we went around the table, each expressing our favorite thing about my stepson as a way to honor him on his birthday. The immediate and unequivocal response from the birthday boy, however, was "NO! I don't want to do that."

Knowing that proceeding in a way imposed by me wouldn't accomplish what I wanted, I let it go, cheerfully saying, "OK." But my intention was out there, and surprisingly, that wasn't the end of it. Someone suggested that perhaps I could say what I was thinking about the birthday boy without requiring everyone else to do so. Everyone listened politely while I expressed, sincerely, what I really appreciated about my stepson, and I wished him a happy and satisfying day. It was a different kind of talk. Then I let it go, again.

The intention I had clarified moments before seemed to get legs and a life of its own at that point. Another family member said, "Hey, I'd like to say something, too."

One by one, everyone around the table honored my stepson with a sincere expression of appreciation for something they liked about him. When we finished speaking, there was a noticeable shift in the energy of the group, leaving us together in a different, more connected way.

This is a precious gift of the Art of Convening.

—Cynthia Wold

TECHNOLOGY OF RELATIONSHIPS

At the foundation of the Art of Convening is a "technology of relationships." If you hold as true that each interaction with another human being is an opportunity for authentic engagement or relationship, that interaction is enhanced. *The Art of Convening* is a guide to help us integrate our personal values into positive relationships that make possible the best outcomes for our gatherings, whether for communities, organizations, or the world.

We use a Convening Wheel model to explore the convergence of the inner and outer worlds of Conveners—those who engage others in meaningful meetings, discourse, and conversations. The integration of the personal practices of the Convener with the practical concerns of convening meetings and gatherings is the unique realm of the Art of Convening.

INNER JOURNEY

We discovered while developing the Convening Wheel that the outer, physical, design-oriented delivery considerations in convening always seem to follow the same path as the inner life of the Convener. That is why the inner considerations are so prominent in our convening model. We believe that the Convener is a leader whose power and effectiveness are rooted in personal development, integrity, and coherence. When we tap into the generosity inherent in most people, the wealth of knowledge and wisdom in any gathering is revealed.

To illustrate the concepts of the Art of Convening, we've developed the Convening Wheel model.

THE CONVENING WHEEL

The Convening Wheel is the form we use to visualize the inner and outer considerations of the Convener. The parts or phases of the Convening Wheel, the center and eight outer points around the perimeter, are called *Aspects*. We start at the center with *At the Heart of the Matter* and then move up, or north, to *Clarifying Intent*, then travel clockwise all the way around to *Commitment to Action*. We follow a path that reflects both the *presence* and *action* of the Convener. The Wheel reveals an intuitive, logical progression of actively engaged relationship.

You may ask, "Do I really have to do all of these steps?" The short answer is: to get the best result, yes; to see an improvement, no. Begin where it makes the most sense, with a commitment to try following the Wheel as your understanding and practice grow.

Despite our best intentions to use the whole Convening Wheel model, we understand that in our everyday world, sometimes an impromptu conversation or gathering surprises us. Sometimes our active lives deliver us to a gathering unprepared;

or we did not call the meeting, so we arrive feeling that nothing can be done to modify or change the meeting form.

Even so, the power and capacity of the Art of Convening will continue to grow and permeate our gatherings as we utilize and practice it when we can. Every time we practice the Art of Convening, we strengthen the habit, much like learning how to drive a car. After a while, our bodies and minds operate in such a way that the doing of it takes less and less of our conscious thought, but we become more and more proficient.

Here are the nine Aspects of the Convening Wheel, with a definition of each:

At the Heart of the Matter. Who I am in relationship with others.

Clarifying Intent. The alignment of our intention with the purpose of our engagement.

The Invitation. A sincere offering to engage that integrates purpose and intent.

Setting Context. Communicating the form, function, and purpose of our engagement and intent.

Creating the Container. Creating the physical and energetic field within which we meet.

Hearing All the Voices. Each person speaks, is heard, and is present and accounted for.

Essential Conversation. Meaningful exchange within an atmosphere of trust.

Creation. Something new that emerges from engagements of shared purpose and trust.

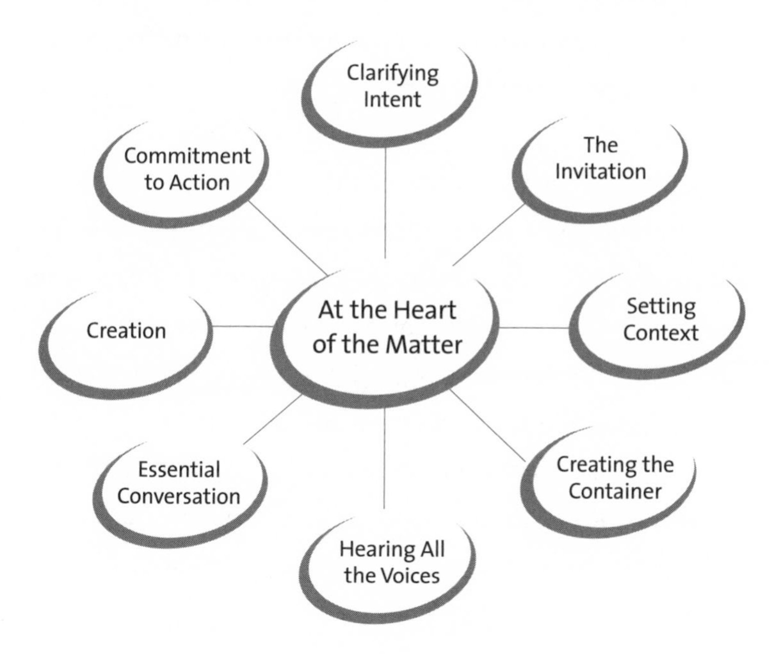

> ***Commitment to Action.*** An individual and/or collective agreement to be responsible and accountable for the way forward.

The structure of the Convening Wheel illustrates the various Aspects of convening as a whole. As we progress through the Aspects around the Wheel (whether tentatively, fitfully, or gracefully), we cycle through the steps and considerations using this circular form to guide our way of being and doing.

The Convening Wheel is flexible. Rather than being limited to a sequential progression, we are able to correct our course at any juncture along the path. As in our individual lives, we at times need to hit the "reset button" to refocus or step back a few paces to a place of balance and equilibrium. This is also true in our relational lives as leaders and Conveners. The path of the Convening Wheel isn't rigid or static any more than are our relationships.

Each of the nine chapters in this book covers an Aspect of the Convening Wheel. Each Aspect builds on the previous and provides a bridge to the next, creating a cycle of wholeness in our relationships and engagements. We examine each by looking at three core elements: the possible Challenge we may face in implementing it, the core Principle behind it, and the Essential Questions that shape our understanding. We also include a "Making It Real" discussion that explores common situations we've come across when engaged in an Aspect of the Convening Wheel.

Here are the definitions of the core elements of each Aspect to further your understanding:

> ***Challenge.*** The fundamental barrier that we must see in order to continue to the next Aspect.
>
> ***Principle.*** The foundational value that informs an Aspect of the Wheel.
>
> ***Essential Questions.*** Questions one asks in an Aspect of the Wheel that illuminate the core Principle.

Each chapter concludes with helpful reminders that summarize the major ideas and themes, including the sections "Aspect-Strengthening Exercises" and "Journaling Questions" for active engagement and practice.

The Art of Convening can produce breakthrough outcomes that are satisfying and extraordinary for the participants as well as their organizations and communities. The guidelines in this book are for those of us seriously engaged in and committed to making a life-changing difference in our own lives and the lives of those we gather.

Through the principles and practices of the Art of Convening, anyone can learn that meaningful connection and engagement are not only possible but also imperative for obtaining sustainable, satisfying results in our businesses, organizations, communities, families, and personal relationships.

The chapters that follow take you through the Aspects one by one while exploring each in detail.

Our gratitude goes out to you for your willingness to step forward with us on the Convener's journey.

—Craig and Patricia Neal

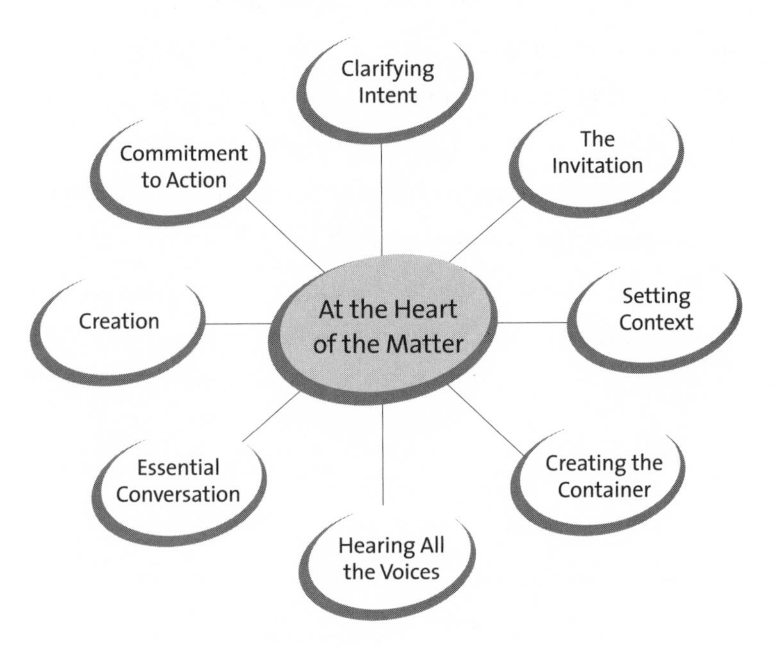
Clarifying Intent
The Invitation
Setting Context
Creating the Container
Hearing All the Voices
Essential Conversation
Creation
Commitment to Action
At the Heart of the Matter

1. AT THE HEART OF THE MATTER

Who I am in relationship with others

WHAT IS *AT THE HEART OF THE MATTER*?

The place to start when we convene meetings, gatherings, and conversations is with ourselves. If we are to lead into authentic engagement, it is important to be genuine. Knowing who we are as human beings helps us to bring this genuineness forward. Additionally, our ability to frame, embody, and model authentic engagement is improved when we explore how we will be in relationship with others.

> AUTHENTIC ENGAGEMENT
> *A genuine expression of what is true for us, and an attentive listening to what is true for another, or others.*

We call this first, central Aspect of the Convening Wheel *At the Heart of the Matter*.

This is where we practice knowing ourselves as human beings and enter an awareness of how we will be in relationship with others. It is a big subject, and a lifelong quest and journey for many of us.

The idea of knowing oneself is the foundational premise of countless leadership books and trainings, as well as other self-improvement, motivational, and spiritual literature. There is a reason for that. It is important. Approaching the principles and practices of the Art of Convening without getting at this core Aspect, one way or another, would be like trying to make a wheel without a hub; it can be done, but, well, that's one wobbly wheel. This central Aspect serves as a stabilizer and calibrator for our convening practice; we return to it again and again.

Many of us are on a continuing journey of self-reflection. What we have learned, and will learn on that journey, will serve us well as Conveners. If we are just beginning a journey of knowing ourselves, a convening practice is one place to start. A difference between *At the Heart of the Matter* and many other journeys of self-reflection is that we also examine how we will be in relationship with others. When we think of these things, we get at the heart of our relationship with the participants of our gathering.

CHALLENGE

Staying connected

Do we choose to open ourselves to relationship, or do we choose to close?

In times of high stress, we can be distracted from our connection to who we are. Convening, for Heartland, is the art of gathering and "holding" people, in a safe and generative space, for the sake of an authentic engagement that works for all. We consider each gathering to be an entry into a relationship with others. Staying authentically connected to others is, ultimately, all about being connected to ourselves. If we are not in touch with ourselves and the core of our intent, how can we maintain a genuine connection to other people?

there is a journey
of the heart
that calls to those
who are seeking
something
more

beyond the well traveled
roads of repeated platitudes
and long held beliefs
there awaits a plentitude
of new ideas yearning
to be explored

out there somewhere
in the realms of what we
don't even know we don't know
lies a vast
vista of possibilities
open to discovery . . .

—Minx Boren[1]

The purpose of *At the Heart of the Matter* is to increase our clarity, confidence, and sense of belonging so that, come what may, we are able to hold others in the safest, most generative container possible. Although personal and internal, this Aspect is a powerful touchstone, and precursor, for thoughtful intention and design of our meetings. Some of the exercises in this book will help us get started or continue to reveal to ourselves who we are, which will increase our ability to stay connected and open to our relationships with others.

PRINCIPLE

Knowing who I am allows me to be in authentic engagement.

Our undertaking to connect with other human beings in a genuine, meaningful way is what authentic engagement is all about. But unless we are willing to reflect on who we are, we don't give others something real to connect to. Expecting to authentically engage with others when we don't know ourselves is like believing that we can physically grasp a hologram or lean on the mist; it seems as if there's something there, but when we try it out, we learn differently.

The journey of self-reflection that we begin or continue with this Aspect of the Convening Wheel provides something solid for us and others to connect to.

FORGING THE INNER HEART

The first container that required attention was the one shaped in my own interior. I needed, for my own sake and for the sake of the whole, to make sure there was a connection between my stated desire for real community and authenticity and my own life. In order for me to lead with integrity, I needed to close the gap between my exterior persona and my interior reality.

In preparation for an important meeting I was to convene, I spent many hours attending to my own fears, assumptions, hopes, freedoms, and limitations. I took long, meditative walks; I journaled; I consulted with colleagues (including my AoC partners). When it came time for the meeting, I was able to hold the group with a sense of nonanxious presence. I cannot overstate how important that was for me and for the gathered whole. I have learned that what happens in the days and hours before the meeting is at least as important as what takes place in the meeting.

Because I attended to my interior container, I was more prepared to help shape an outer container—in the context of the meeting—large enough to hold the charged emotional engagements of the group.

—By Terry Chapman[2]

ESSENTIAL QUESTIONS

Who am I as a human being?

How will I be in relationship with others?

When we have thoroughly explored these questions, the connection of ourselves in relationship to others makes more sense and tends to flow more naturally. When we practice mindful reminders through reflective practices, we bring ourselves back to our basic humanity.

These are internal reflections. Whether we share our discovery with others is not as important as truthfully addressing these questions for ourselves. Our discovery will be *At the Heart of the Matter*. The journaling questions and exercises at the end of the chapter will help focus our internal vision in order to explore these questions.

Through this internal inquiry, we have the opportunity to experience the core of *who we are* and *how we will be* in relationship with others. When we understand the nature of why we desire to be in relationship with others, our gatherings tend to have an integrity that goes beyond the sole reliance on form and technique. This quality allows for the possibility of authentic connection.

As Terry pointed out in "Forging the Inner Heart," spending hours attending to his own internal condition was essential. This enabled him, when the time came, to be centered, grounded, and able to "hold the group with a sense of nonanxious presence."

MAKING IT REAL

There is a lot of pressure in our lives to go, go, go all the time—to drive results and spring into action, often before the action's optimal time has come. It's counterintuitive to take the time to reflect on how we will be in relationship with others. In a way, we have to slow down and do the internal due diligence to know what results we really want to drive and when it is time to take an action.

This Aspect of the Convening Wheel is all about remembering who we are—perhaps recalling the person we forgot we were, in all the hubbub of life and work.

> TRUE LEADERSHIP
> *is an inside job.*
> —*Michael Bush*[3]

Some of us may already have a practice that sufficiently serves the purpose of spurring self-examination and self-knowledge. If we don't have a practice or want to add to what we already do, there are practices, both ancient and modern, that can help us remember. An ongoing practice of self-reflection, of any kind, is a potent tool for getting *At the Heart of the Matter*, and can enable us to be better prepared in whatever conditions we convene.

Practices of remembering, such as meditation, prayer, reflection, journal keeping, walks in nature, and contemplation, are very helpful. When we begin to lose our self-awareness, find ourselves in a state of stress and confusion, or want to reinforce what we already know, we can strengthen *At the Heart of the Matter* using them. These practices help to focus our thoughts and strengthen our sense of presence in the moment, allowing us to enter into authentic engagements with confidence.

Mindfulness: Mindfulness and meditative practices are designed to bring the mind, body, and emotions to relaxation, thus allowing us to approach whatever is next refreshed, present, and fully awake. A mindfulness exercise is included at the end of this chapter.

Prayer: Prayer is expressing our relationship with a higher power, and there are as many ways to pray as there are religions and belief systems. The contemplative nature of prayer has an effect of bringing one closer to one's true self.

Conscious reflection: Creating time, no matter how busy or distracted we may be, to focus our attention on the positive aspects of our lives is conscious reflection. Taking time to consider, with gratitude and appreciation, is a competency that can bring us to a more generative mindset.

Journal keeping: The act of journaling often reveals our own wisdom. It can be helpful to journal (or write by hand, computer, or other device) our thoughts at particular times when we are moved or when we want to discover something inside ourselves.

Contemplation: To contemplate something is to focus our thoughts exclusively on that thing. We use this practice to turn down the noise and see the main subject of our thoughts clearly.

Spending time in nature: In this context, the purpose of being in nature is to immerse ourselves in the biological world, where we all come from and to which we all belong. Often the beauty and presence of nature enables us to become more fully aware of our connections to life.

We take a "time in" when we use the practices above to make room in our minds and hearts for an awareness of what is *At the Heart of the Matter* to emerge. We may draw on any number of practices at various times until we are satisfied with the outcome.

When we enter into relationships with those we gather, from the firm ground that comes from self-reflection, we have confidence, courage, and a sense of what is possible. Our capacity for authentic engagement is increased as we frame, embody, and model this kind of connection, and give others something real to connect to.

This is the beginning of our journey around the Convening Wheel. We complete this Aspect by exploring who we are and how we will be in relationship with others. Each interaction with another human being is an opportunity for relationship; awareness of that fact creates a shift in our interactions. The journey that begins here is a powerful way to bring authentic engagement to meetings, gatherings, and conversations because knowing who we are in relationship with others is a sustaining force that keeps the Convening Wheel together.

ELEPHANTS AND AUTHENTICITY

I convened a gathering of 150 executives at a state social services agency. The initial request was to facilitate a daylong offsite retreat, to engage in a five-year visioning process, that would create a high level of participant input, feedback, and agreement on a way forward, in difficult times, for the agency. The desired outcome would be a five-year vision statement to be distributed throughout the organization.

A week before the event, a series of dramatic budget cuts, personnel changes, and presenter shifts were made. It was decided that we would go ahead with the retreat in the midst of these changes. However, our initial design of this event had been figuratively ripped away.

How would I proceed now that this additional emotional stress and uncertainty factor had been added to the equation?

I began to look to others for guidance—to tell me who I needed to be for this gathering and how I could be in relationship with the people there when emotions might be running exceptionally high. I found that the more I looked to others for the answer, the more confused I became.

Several days before the retreat, I consciously engaged in a series of reflective practices that helped focus my energies and get *At the Heart of the Matter*. Setting aside some time alone to meditate, I visualized the gathering and imagined the best possible outcome. This practice of envisioning myself and others authentically engaged allowed me to see my way forward step by step. I wrote in my journal to put substance to my thoughts, intents, and outcomes, which made my vision more real to me—and enabled me to share some of my discoveries with others. These practices allowed me to articulate who I am as a human being and how I would be in relationship with others, grounding my emotions and enabling me to imagine the most powerful and beneficial outcome possible with the other designers for the retreat.

By grounding myself through a self-reflective process, I returned to the core of why I had entered the agreement to convene this session. Once I embodied the truth of what was *At the Heart of the Matter*, a sense of confidence, purpose, and courage to step into the unknown guided me forward.

I came to a place of nonjudgment where trusting myself was the important touchstone that would carry my relationship with the others at this gathering and would bring much-needed authenticity to this retreat.

What had come to me out of this process was that before we could envision the way forward, we needed to speak honestly and clearly about the present condition, which had yet to be done.

As I entered the room that morning, my intuition told me that the day would flow seamlessly. The design and production teams and those that came early seemed to sense this positive energy right away. I gathered the design team about an hour before the start of the retreat to say that we had a very powerful design and that all we needed to do now was to welcome people and tell the truth as we knew it.

There were several elephants in the room, known as budget cuts, layoffs, and wholesale destruction of the department. At my request, we began by having the two core presenters agree to speak openly and honestly about three questions: what did they know that they could say, what would be the impact on the department, and, more important, how did they feel at this moment—how did this affect them?

We had chosen to remain open to relationship with the people in that room. The presenters were willing to authentically engage. We were all willing to say what was true for us. You could feel the cloud lifting, the stress leaving the room, the space opening to authentic possibility, and a visceral leaning forward of each person to take part in an active way because they felt an invitation to be real.

—By Craig Neal

Where We Are on the Convening Wheel

1. *At the Heart of the Matter*—We have explored who we are and how we will be in relationship with others.

We have started the journey. Now we are ready to proceed to an exciting and crucial Aspect for the gathering at hand, *Clarifying Intent.*

Things to Remember

Challenge: *Staying connected—Do we choose to open ourselves to relationship or do we choose to close?*

Principle: *Knowing who I am allows me to be in authentic engagement.*

Essential Questions:

- Who am I as a human being?
- How will I be in relationship with others?

Aspect-Strengthening Exercises

Checklist for the Gathering at Hand

- Who am I in relationship to this gathering?
- What is my relationship to the people of this gathering?
- What is the purpose of our gathering?
- What does success look like?
- Have I centered myself (noticed my preferences, judgments, and certainties)?
- Am I ready to move on? (If not, why not?)

Practices-of-Remembering Exercises

Mindfulness: Choose a quiet, dark, or softly lit place to sit, either in a chair or on the floor/ground. Close your eyes or gaze softly at an object ahead. Now, shift your attention to your breath and simply notice the thoughts that come up and the sounds around you while letting them pass by. Allow yourself a few minutes at first; you may wish to increase the time as it suits you.

For more on mindfulness practice, see *Mindfulness Meditation: Cultivating the Wisdom of Your Body and Mind,* by Jon Kabat-Zinn (Nightingale-Conant, 2002).

Prayer: *I like to start my day with a walking prayer of about one hour. The first 15 minutes or so, my mind wanders to the things of the coming day that draw my attention. Then I enter a time when I am able to gently let go and just be with what is. I notice the surroundings, my own breath, and I begin to feel the rhythm of the walk. Often, other thoughts come to mind: mostly gratitude for life, gratitude for the beauty of creation, and a sense of grounding. As my mind and body open, people come to mind. I hold them there in this place of nonanxious presence and think about their lives, sending them love. Some may call this a prayer of intercession. For me, it is an opening into my essential self, which then creates a posture of being present to the world.*

—Terry Chapman[4]

Conscious reflection:

1. Find a comfortable place to sit with your feet on the floor and hands in your lap.
2. If you're comfortable to do so, close your eyes and notice your breathing. Otherwise, just soften your gaze.
3. Shift your focus away from your mind to the area around your heart.
4. Imagine yourself breathing through your heart. It may help to put your hand on your heart.
5. Keep your focus there for 10 seconds or more.
6. Now, recall a time in which you felt appreciation for someone or something and attempt to reexperience it.
7. Notice the feeling.
8. When you're ready, open your eyes.[5]

Contemplation: *To contemplate is to find a place in one's being for stillness. This does not come easy for busy people. But with practice, one discovers a place of stillness, just under the surface of our often frenetic lives. The 20th-century Jewish mystic Abraham Heschel wrote of such a place: "In the tempestuous ocean of time and toil there are islands of stillness where we may enter a harbor and reclaim our dignity." At the* *end of the day, in a quiet, spacious place, consider the movements of the day. Reflect on times when you felt a tightness in your chest, anxiety, cynicism, or even fear. Name those experiences and gently let them go. Then also intentionally recall moments in the day when you felt peace, joy, centeredness, and attunement. Give thanks for those moments and hold them for a while in your mind. This practice of sifting through the moments of the day can help focus the heart and mind so that one can let go of that which may be harmful, and hold on to that which brings more life.*

—Terry Chapman[6]

EXERCISE 1: WHAT DO I STAND FOR?

The set-up:

You can do this in 20 minutes.

Find a quiet place to write, and close the door so that you won't be interrupted.

Write by hand (or computer if you must) in your journal. Any notebook will do as long as you know it will remain private.

Step 1. Who are the people who most influenced your life—positively or negatively? List them by name and by their relationship to you. You may wish to express why they are influential; however, this is not required. Once you've finished, pause to reflect on each before moving on to Step 2.

Step 2. *What are the core nonnegotiable values that guide your life and work?* Ask yourself about the bedrock values that guide you in your life and work. List key words first, noticing how they feel. You may have only a few; don't worry. It's more important that you find those that are not open to negotiation to you and that reflect how you live your life.

Step 3. *Share those values with someone as soon as possible.* Start by saying, "I stand for [the values you've written down] in my life and work."

Step 4 (optional). *Write a short narrative story that is declarative.* It starts with "I" and goes on from there. Something like this: "I stand for integrity and love in all my relations. My family is sacred to me. Truth, humor, and play are essential to my daily life. My body is my temple and I take care of it . . ."

EXERCISE 2: A PERSONAL CREATION STORY

Personal creation stories are a powerful tool to attract what we desire to create in our lives. When we can envision our future, we are more likely to create the changes, put forth the effort, and acquire the skills necessary to achieve it. This is also a good way to explore who we are and how we will be in relationship with others.

What to do: Write a one-page creation story for yourself as a Convener, a gatherer and holder of people, for the next two years.

Step 1. Find a quiet place to reflect and write with no distractions. Allow yourself at least 30 minutes for each writing session.

Step 2. Once seated, ask yourself these simple yet potent questions:

- What is next for my life, and how can I consciously create what I want? (List events, things you want to accomplish, changes you wish to see for yourself, and so on.)
- What do I need to leave behind in order to do that? (List those things that are in the way of your actualizing what you desire.)

Step 3. Now imagine yourself two years out: What do you see for yourself? What are you doing? Write a one-page story or narrative to yourself in the first person. For example, "I am happily living in ___ with ___, having just made a decision to pursue my passion by ___ (date or time)," and so forth.

Some focusing questions to help you get started:

- What is the story that I tell others about myself as a Convener?
- Who am I in relationship with others, and why do I authentically engage?
- What calls me to convene?

Journaling Questions

- What are my relationships now, and how do I serve?
- What is my vision for myself as a Convener? Write the story of your life two years out. List accomplishments and/or milestones. Be specific.

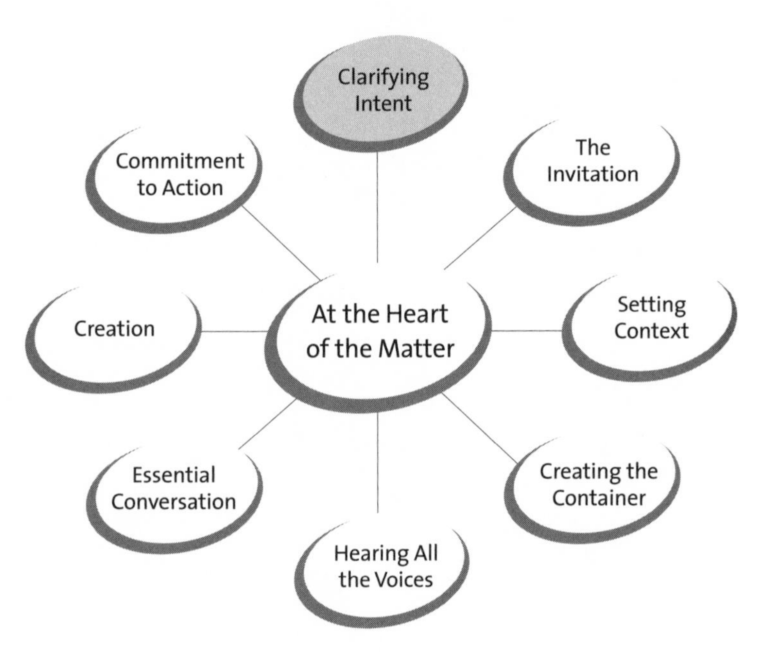
Clarifying Intent
The Invitation
Setting Context
Creating the Container
Hearing All the Voices
Essential Conversation
Creation
Commitment to Action
At the Heart of the Matter

2. CLARIFYING INTENT

The alignment of our intention with the purpose of our engagement

WHAT IS INTENTION?

Our intention is the result that we desire for our actions, words, and/or presence to have in the world. Sometimes we are aware of these desires, and sometimes we are not. *Clarifying Intent* is essential for a gathering because our intentions have substance that will be acted upon.

> THE INTENTION *for, and orientation to, the highest good for each and all serves as our fundamental and ever-present touchstone. It is an invocation more than an agenda, a powerful tone that reverberates through visible and invisible realms to attract all who support our effort. Clear strong intent is a potent attractor in the field of Being.*
>
> —*Tom Hurley*[1]

In the last chapter, we examined *At the Heart of the Matter*, reflecting on who we are and how we will be in relationship with other people. Now we engage in *Clarifying Intent* for the gathering at hand. For the best outcome of our gathering to be possible, our intentions must also be in alignment with *At the Heart of the Matter*.

Often, our intentions for a gathering, if not examined, can be confused, conflicting, and sometimes even unknown. We engage in the practice of *Clarifying Intent* so that we can better identify any or all of our intentions and deliberately choose intentions that are in alignment with who we are and how we will be in relationship with others. Once we have done this, undesirable intentions or motives lose power, and our desired, embraced, and invoked intention begins its work of attracting internal and external allies and energy.

CHALLENGE

Doubt

The primary barrier we struggle with in this Aspect is doubt. Doubt is a subtle form of fear and can derail our attempt to *clarify our intent*. Doubt may show up as the cynical belief that as long as we put on a pleasant face and plow through our gathering, true intentions don't matter. Or it may show up as the belief that underlying motives make no difference as long as we keep them invisible to ourselves and/or others.

> MY DEEPEST *intention is always to serve, to encourage healing (in the meaning of fostering wholeness) and to embody love. I realized over time that by setting a clear intention for each gathering, for each day—I unleashed an energetic field which then drew the outer physical manifestation of that intention to me as I simultaneously was making my way towards "it."*
>
> *—Pele Rouge Chadima*[2]

Much of our communication is nonverbal. As when a musical note is not quite in tune, if purpose is not aligned with our intent and action, people may not be able to put their finger on the discord, yet that still small voice inside each of us perceives this imbalance when it occurs. This dissonance has been the killer of countless meeting agendas in the early stages of development.

Once we engage in a practice of examining our intentions and fearlessly identifying them, we have a conscious choice to move forward or not. The power of any undesirable intentions diminishes as they are seen, recognized, and deliberately set aside. The power of desirable intentions that are in alignment with who we are increases as we consciously embrace and communicate them. Our own fully embraced intention feeds our power to actualize it.

PRINCIPLE

Our intent has substance that is acted upon.

In order to appreciate the importance of this Aspect, we understand that our intentions—whether or not we communicate them—really do have substance, are perceived and grasped by others, and are acted upon.

When we call a meeting or extend an invitation to another individual for a gathering, various motives or intentions can be present outside our awareness. Yet often we operate on autopilot, taking for granted that our ostensible intentions, stated or unstated, are clear to ourselves and to others.

Some of the stories we hear from Art of Convening participants about *Clarifying Intent* involve confusion about conflicting intentions or with finding some underlying motives that the Convener does not consciously want to bring into the gathering.

Some people have recognized failures in their gathering as the direct result of not *Clarifying Intent.*

One past Art of Convening participant told of a coworker's seemingly mystifying angry reaction to her innocent attempt to offer helpful feedback in a conversation. Later, she admitted that she had unacknowledged "issues" with that person, and although she did not consciously intend harm, the offer of feedback had not been made with innocent goodwill. She reported that the exercise of *Clarifying Intent* would have allowed her to understand, identify, and set aside any of her ulterior motives in that conversation, and to move forward with a primary intention of authentic engagement and improved relationship.

The utility of *Clarifying Intent* lies in our ability to identify and clearly understand an intention for our gathering, an intention that is fully in alignment with *At the Heart of the Matter* and that we consciously embrace. When we *clarify intent,* we also invoke something in ourselves, in others, and in the universe that is ready to invest in our intention, making it more likely that our engagement will be successful.

> *What matters and what counts*
> *are imagination and inspiration,*
> *a "Hail Yes!" we can attitude,*
> *and a roll up our sleeves movement*
> *of such magnitude that the future*
> *can hear us coming*
> *with our heads held high*
> *above the cloudy predictions*
> *and our knapsacks filled with*
> *our gumption and our grit*
> *our gifts and our gratitudes—*
> *the building blocks of new*
> *cornerstones of possibility.*
>
> —*Minx Boren*[3]

ESSENTIAL QUESTIONS

What are my intentions?

Are they in line with who I am?

Who are we to be together?

These Essential Questions require us to remain in the "being" realm of convening. With these questions, we bring into play our relationship with others: *who* we are to be, and then *how* we are to be with one another. From these reflections flows the recognition of an intention that will have substance. With a clarified personal intent to be engaged, the design of the gathering and how it will be executed unfolds more easily. *The Invitation*, the third Aspect, is the logical next step in articulating our purpose and intent.

If our intention is muddy, confused, or ambiguous, it may eventually be revealed in a wishy-washy *Invitation* or as resistance to our stated vision.

WILDERNESS BONDING

For many years—as a boy and a young man—I was drawn to the wilderness. When my sons reached the age where they could hold their own on a camping trip into the Boundary Waters Canoe Area of northern Minnesota, we began what has become a father-and-son journey into ourselves through the beauty and solitude of the wilderness. The time away from our usual demanding lives in the city refreshed and renewed not only our bodies and minds, but even more important, our relationship. We became friends and confidants around the campfire, and that has brought a depth in trust and intimacy we may never have known.

In order to get to that place for myself, it was very helpful to have thought through the real purpose and intent of why I wanted this trip for my sons and myself. It might seem as if a father-son camping gathering needs no internal preparation. "They're my children, I say we're going, and we go." Many outings are reasonably successful with just that. But I really wanted to have a bonding experience that was meaningful for all of us, and so I spent some time thinking about that.

This was before I formulated the Convening Wheel, but the inkling that there was something powerful in my intentions was still a factor in the way I did things.

When I thought deeply about what my intention was for taking my sons to the BWCA, surprisingly, many motives showed up. My main intention, which was in alignment with my heart, was to bond with my sons and strengthen our relationship. What surprised me were the other motives that I had not acknowledged: showing my sons my expertise in the wilderness, impressing them with my skill, showing them how to do the things that I could do, and seeing them appreciate the beauty of the land. These weren't bad motives or intentions, but I really had to work at setting them aside so that the energy of our trip would focus on that one main, important motive: strengthening the relationship with my sons.

I had engaged in *Clarifying Intent* without knowing it.

Once I made it clear to myself what my main, aligned intention was, and acknowledged—but set aside—the other motives for this trip, it seemed as if things came together internally and externally to make this bonding possible.

I was able to let go of any preconceived notions of what the boys would be like on the journey. It didn't matter that much whether or not they paddled the canoe a certain way or appreciated the land as much as I did. I could do this because I had *clarified my intention* and acknowledged these things as distractions from my main, aligned intent.

The result was better than I could have imagined, and my relationship with my sons was greatly improved.

—By Craig Neal

MAKING IT REAL

We've all experienced how distractions that seem important in the moment can cause our gatherings to flounder. If we *clarify our intent,* we have the opportunity to get crystal-clear about what really matters in our gathering. We can then navigate the waters of distraction by remembering our true intent. This does the work of resetting our compass and adjusting our course when the wind and current push us this way and that. If we don't do this, we may find ourselves setting out for China and winding up in New Zealand.

We have found that to bring authentic engagement to our gatherings, it is helpful to *intend* to have authentic engagement. This one intention, or awareness, can sometimes hold a group together.

To *clarify our intentions,* we identify those motives or desires that might distract us or others from what is primary. In order to do this, we search inside ourselves. Clarification involves sifting out what isn't wanted and needed. As Craig tells in his story about going to the wilderness with his sons, acknowledging and mentally setting aside motives that could distract from his main intention was an important exercise. It allowed that father-son gathering to unfold in a way that kept them headed toward bonding, which was his primary intent.

Staying in the self-reflective mode is challenging. It requires patience if we are to deepen our sense of conviction and commitment to our own inner authority, which will lead to clear intent. If we are to maximize the depth and effectiveness of our engagements, the patience to hold off the impulse to move into premature conclusions may enable us to bring the fully developed gift of our intention into a thoroughly considered invitation to engage.

Once examined, our deepest intent has power and force that, in its natural progression around the Wheel, will find its way into action.

The tendency for many is to move too quickly from the heart to the head and then to the outcome. The preparatory work of actualizing the intention we have for ourselves in relationship with others is necessary before we go further with commitment and confidence.

When we design our meeting or gathering, our intention takes on energy that operates outside of our direct control. This energy will sometimes bring in essential elements that we hadn't realized were essential.

SHEDDING LIGHT BY INTENT

Recently I organized a breakout session on resource management within R&D at our company—a topic fraught with internal politics and competing needs. I believe that the intention of a meeting is the force that guides and shapes its unfolding. It originates from the Convener and needs to be communicated to and supported by attendees. If the intention is not clear or not sufficiently supported, then the meeting will likely drift and feel ineffective or unsatisfying.

In this meeting, my intent was to shed light on the dynamics involved in asking the group to explore the "voices of the system," to identify the different categories of people involved in resource management decisions, and then to articulate what they thought was going on in their minds as they made these decisions. What were their interests and concerns? I had never led a session like this and was concerned that some might find it confusing.

I did not have to achieve a specific outcome. My intention was primarily to create an encouraging and supportive environment that would enable people to explore the voices of the system. I wanted it to be fun and energizing, and to offer an expanded view of the dynamics involved in these decisions. My intention as facilitator was to be confident, relaxed, attentive, and trusting.

I didn't know, specifically, what would be needed to make this happen, but my intention was very clear to me, and I reminded myself of that primary intention throughout the meeting so that I would not be distracted from it. I remained confident and trusting, even when presented with a diverse range of interests, and even after making a dramatic change to the meeting format on the fly.

The session successfully achieved the primary intention of providing people with an expanded view of the system, and did so in a fun and energizing way. I know that taking the time to clarify my intention for this gathering made a difference in how it unfolded and what was achieved.

—By Eric Babinet[4]

Where We Are on the Convening Wheel

1. *At the Heart of the Matter*—We have explored who we are and how we will be in relationship with others.
2. *Clarifying Intent*—We have identified an intention consistent with *At the Heart of the Matter* that has substance and is acted upon.

Now that we have *clarified intent*, we are ready, with confidence, to extend the *Invitation*.

Things to Remember

Challenge: *Doubt. Do we have confidence in ourselves as we move forward?*

Principle: *Our intent has substance that is acted upon.*

Essential Questions:

- What are my intentions?
- Are they in line with who I am?
- Who are we to be together?

Aspect-Strengthening Exercises

Checklist for the Gathering at Hand

- Are my intentions in alignment with my core values?
- Do I have confidence that this engagement is worthwhile and doable?
- Have I given enough attention to a design that actualizes my intention?
- Who is coming, and have I designed with them in mind?

EXERCISE: ON INTENT

The set-up: Find a quiet place to reflect and write with no distractions. Allow yourself at least 30 minutes for each writing session.

The assumptions:

- Be fully awake to the present moment.
- Be a conduit and catalyst for your own truth and authenticity.
- Know that life is an unfolding journey in which you are ready and prepared to engage.
- Know that everyone is whole and perfect just as they are.
- Know that convening is the art of relationship.

Step 1. Ask yourself the (Alice and the Caterpillar) question: Who are you? And what are you doing right now?

Step 2. Write an intention for your next meeting or gathering that takes some or all of this knowing into consideration. Hint: remember Eric's story and how he set an intention for the design and outcomes for the group and himself.

Journaling Questions

- When you think of the word *intent* from this chapter, what words, thoughts, feelings, come up for you? Are they in line with who you are?
- What are the practices you employ in your life to help clarify your intent?

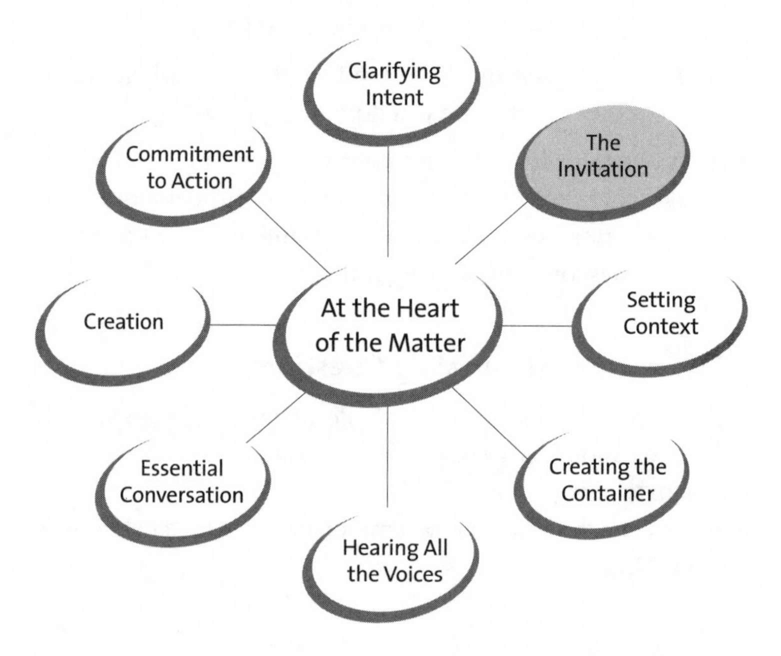
Clarifying Intent
The Invitation
Setting Context
Creating the Container
Hearing All the Voices
Essential Conversation
Creation
Commitment to Action
At the Heart of the Matter

3. THE INVITATION

A sincere offering to engage that integrates purpose and intent

WHAT IS AN AUTHENTIC INVITATION?

Once we have explored the nature of our purpose in *At the Heart of the Matter,* and have clearly identified and aligned the intention for our gathering by *Clarifying Intent,* we again look inside ourselves so that a sincere invitation can be extended. Although important, the physical form of an invitation is simply the delivery system of this Aspect. The essential and often-overlooked quality needed to make an invitation effective is sincerity.

When we convene, our *Invitation* does not just ask for a body to show up at a date and time. It is designed for authentic engagement—to create the opportunity for those invited to bring themselves *fully present,* both when they arrive and continually throughout the gathering. We invite that presence through the sincere tone and warmth of our *Invitation.* When participants have received this kind of invitation, there is a better chance that they will show up physically, and a much better chance that they will arrive with *presence,* ready to participate fully in the gathering.

GENUINE HOSPITALITY, GENEROSITY, AND CONVICTION

We integrate our purpose and formulate a clear intent to create the first social or outer expression as a Convener. Although much of what we will examine about the *Invitation* is still internal to the Convener, with the expression/extension of the *Invitation*, we take the step into actualizing active relationship, which will be reflected in the quality of the *Invitation*.

> THE INVITATION *is about participation, not mere observation. We are not journeying in the universe but with the universe. We are not concerned about living in an evolving world but co-evolving with our world. We are parts of a whole, much greater than the sum of its parts, and yet within each part we are interconnected with the whole.*
>
> —*Diarmuid O'Murchu*[1]

In our socially complex world, invitations can be complicated. We invite people formally or informally, using the vehicles of voice (in person or via phone), e-mail, online invitation websites, postal mail, fliers, media announcements, or hand-delivered notes, to name a few.

No matter what the form, the *Invitation* is extended with genuine hospitality, generosity, and conviction. Anticipation of rejection can sometimes interfere with our willingness to wholeheartedly invite others, but the likelihood of rejection increases when we don't invite this way.

When our *Invitation* is made with genuine hospitality, generosity, and conviction, all manner of possibilities open to the meeting.

- We are *hospitable* when we extend our welcome to the recipient of our *Invitation* with sincerity. The gesture is the open arms.
- We are *generous* when we offer the full warmth and resources of the gathering environment. The gesture is the open hands.
- We have *conviction* when we invite in such a way that recipients are convinced of the value of their presence at the meeting or gathering. The gesture is the sincere, open smile.

Imagine open arms, open hands, and open smile together as the gesture of sincere invitation. This gesture communicates openness to relationship and can be demonstrated via our body language when we greet in person, or through our voice and tone as we imagine ourselves using this gesture when greeting people virtually.

CHALLENGE

Rejection

A primary challenge we invariably confront in order to extend a full, wholehearted, and sincere invitation is the anticipation of rejection. It takes some courage to offer our whole heart in a sincere request when others are free to refuse. Paradoxically, when we withhold our wholehearted invitation, the likelihood of refusal increases.

When we design our *Invitation*, therefore, we revisit *At the Heart of the Matter* and *Clarifying Intent*. Our good intentions and knowledge of who we will be in relationship with others will support a confident, sincere request, knowing rejection as just another form of freedom, not to be feared.

The rejection of an invitation to engage may be the door opener to an even deeper level of relationship, once a future invitation is accepted.

PRINCIPLE

The combination of sincerity, hospitality, and generosity is a strong attractor for full presence.

The objective of our *Invitation* is not just to get people to show up, but also to create the opportunity for them *to be fully present and contribute their gifts*. When people who attend experience that their presence is truly wanted and valuable, and that their unique gift is necessary for the best outcome of the gathering, the possibility for authentic engagement, leading to success, is greatly enhanced.

For an event, especially a business or social appointment, the invitation for engagement creates a promise that is freely made and carries an obligation to do something together.

> INVITATION IS *the means through which hospitality is created. Invitation counters the conventional belief that change requires mandate or persuasion. Invitation honors the importance of choice, the necessary condition for accountability.*
>
> —Peter Block[2]

When we extend an invitation, our communication to the recipient is, "I want you to attend because you have something to offer." Once we are committed to extending an invitation, the sincerity and clarity of our intent, as well as the message, are essential. Our genuine desire for relationship will be communicated in our *Invitation*—yes, even to those we think may have to be invited for political, relational, or hierarchical reasons.

ESSENTIAL QUESTIONS

Who am I to invite?

What is at the heart of my invitation?

Why should they come?

These questions align our heart with our intent. If we don't do this internal work, our invitation may come off as halfhearted and/or insincere. Most of us have been on the receiving end of this sort of invitation. We may politely decline, or we may just not attend. If we do decide to come, we often arrive tentatively and likely are not fully present.

INVITING FULL PRESENCE

Sandra, a senior executive in a large corporation, reported that the Art of Convening model provided transformational success in the project of "breaking down silos," an identified goal of her organization.

After taking the Art of Convening training, she had decided to approach a meeting across departments under her direction using the Convening Wheel. She prepared herself first, clarifying her intention of bringing the group members into authentic engagement for the purpose of understanding their connection to each other so that they could work with a "We're all in this together" attitude. As the boss, she just had to require people to come. But she thought further about what it meant to be invited.

Because of some difficult conflicts she had encountered in the past and continuing struggles with some of the personalities involved, it took some deeper thinking for her to imagine each of the department heads as an individual with unique, needed gifts. There was one person in particular whom she secretly wished would not be available for the meeting because his abrasive style had alienated others in the past.

As Sandra thought of the people she wanted to invite to this meeting, she imagined each as a valuable contributor and began to experience a sincere desire for each individual to attend, regardless of what her previous expectations had been.

In addition to issuing a group memo with an agenda, requiring attendance at the meeting, Sandra decided to write a personal e-mail to each of the eight department heads. She extended an invitation that went beyond requiring. She wrote a sincere note of appreciation to each, and not only asked for their physical presence, but requested, quite genuinely, that each show up prepared to fulfill the promise of his or her own considerable talents, convictions, and creativity.

Sandra reported that everyone came to the meeting (no surprise there). She wasn't quite sure whether the department heads were more open than they would otherwise have been, or if she had just perceived them that way, but there were breakthroughs that day. She had been prepared to engage in the usual refereeing between some strong personalities, but instead was astonished to find a willingness to speak, and listen, with genuine interest and respect. It was not all smooth sailing, but the meeting went remarkably better than she had learned to expect.

For her, the internal preparation she had done beforehand made a difference that was relayed in the sincere invitation she extended. It was the pivotal point that allowed these leaders to come together and authentically engage, as was needed for the project at hand.[3]

MAKING IT REAL

The possibility of rejection is always present when we extend an invitation. A few simple practices can greatly reduce the interference of the anticipation of rejection in our sincere invitation. One is to practice extending sincere invitations and hospitality in our everyday lives, making it a part of *who we are*. This practice hones our sensitivity to the other and helps us to experience the inherent eagerness of others to accept our invitation. It could also be a practice of sending cards or other types of communications to others in order to invite closeness or friendship.

Another practice is to set the table for our family at mealtimes, inviting them to join us for meals. This very simple practice has the twofold effect of increasing our sensitivity to creating an "inviting" place for our gathering, as well as providing practice in extending hospitality.

We invite others to join us for activities, meals, and fellowship even if they have said no in the past, and even if we don't expect them to reciprocate. We send cards to our friends even if they don't send cards back. In this way, we establish who we are and that our desire to engage with others does not depend on their response. Thus the experience of rejection becomes, for us, another form of freedom—not to be feared.

"SHALL WE SALON?"

We launched the *Utne Reader* salon movement in 1991 with a cover story whose headline read, "Salons: How to revive the endangered art of conversation and start a revolution in your living room." Toward the back of the same issue we ran a little ad with the inviting question, "Shall We Salon?" The ad went on to ask, "Would you like to meet up to 25 other people in your neighborhood (town, bioregion) who read *Utne Reader*? Maybe get together with them and have a salon, start a study circle, organize a council, or whatever? If so, send us your name and address, or simply send the mailing label from your current issue of *Utne Reader* to us by April 15, 1991." After a couple of short paragraphs about what respondents could expect, we concluded the ad with Margaret Mead's now-famous lines, "Never doubt that a small group of thoughtful, committed citizens can change the world. Indeed, it's the only thing that ever has."

The ad attracted over 8,200 responses, and we set up 500 salons of up to 20 people in cities all across North America. Within a year, more than 18,000 people had joined the Neighborhood Salon Association, meeting at least monthly in office conference rooms, church basements, coffee shops, and, mostly, each other's living rooms. The Blue Man Group members met each other and formed in an Utne Salon. Countless marriages, businesses, and nonprofit initiatives got their start there, too. Several schools and cohousing projects trace their genesis to Utne Salons. Shortly after the issue came out, a number of large daily newspapers, including all 77 properties in the Gannett newspaper chain, started discussion circles for their readers. The salon movement was born.

The key to the success of our invitation was our assumption that if we were feeling something, our readers must be feeling it, too. Our need for community, to connect with others who shared our interests, values, and concerns, created an offer and invitation that was a sincere expression of a genuine desire.

—*By Eric Utne*[4]

Craig was publisher of *Utne Reader* during the launch of the Neighborhood Salon Association. Crafting a genuine, well-articulated invitation had power and attraction and, for the magazine, was a marriage of social activism, community, and successful business.

REINFORCING OUR SINCERITY

A convening practice we use at Heartland is to read each participant's name out loud prior to a gathering. Quite often the names are read the night before, and sometimes they're read the day of. This process has multiple benefits for the gathering, including the reinforcement of the sincerity of our *Invitation*. As the names are read (either by the Convener alone or by a team), we envision each person as welcome to the meeting, ready to share his or her valuable gifts. It is our experience that this simple practice of quietly honoring each participant produces big rewards. It translates into a genuine expression of appreciation as we go forward with the gathering. See Exercise 1 at the end of this chapter for a full explanation.

The presence we bring as we invite and welcome people into a meeting or gathering is important. When we model the values of hospitality, generosity, and conviction, there is a natural tendency for those in attendance to mirror back those values in kind.

The following example of welcoming by Sheila Hines Edmondson is a fitting illustration of these principles of sincerity and hospitality.

THE OPEN WELCOME

The sincere welcome is an open gesture of goodwill to receive and accept participants upon arrival, acknowledging their place in the event wherever they are on their journey. The welcome puts people at ease. It sets the tone for the activities that will follow in any meeting or gathering.

At a Thought Leader Gathering, for instance, my intention is to create the sense of community and belonging—especially for those who are arriving for the first time—and help them to understand a little about what the process is for our time together.

What I've experienced in response to the welcome has been mixed, but positive. Some may wonder if they are in the right place, because the welcome is much different than at other meetings or events they have attended. There are members of the community who return often and share that they look forward to the greeting. Whether I help make someone's day or not, I'll never know. I do know that my aim is to contribute positively to each person's experience. Our relationship begins with my intention and the greeting.

—By Sheila Hines Edmondson[5]

The *Invitation* is more than perfunctory words on a page or in an e-mail. It includes the internal condition of the one who does the inviting, as well as the form and wording of the actual invitation. Beyond that, the follow-through of our welcome and hospitality from the beginning, and throughout our engagement, makes the *Invitation* a potent attractor for presence.

Where We Are on the Convening Wheel

1. *At the Heart of the Matter*—We have explored who we are and how we will be in relationship with others.
2. *Clarifying Intent*—We have identified an intention consistent with *At the Heart of the Matter* that has substance and is acted upon.
3. *The Invitation*—We have extended a sincere invitation with genuine hospitality, generosity, and conviction.

Now that we have designed and extended the *Invitation* with grace and confidence, we have completed the first third of the Convening Wheel. As we continue to the next Aspect of the Wheel, we will shift the concern to *Setting Context*.

Things to Remember

Challenge: *Rejection*

Principle: *The combination of sincerity, hospitality, and generosity is a strong attractor for full presence.*

Essential Questions:

- Who am I to invite?
- What is at the heart of my invitation?
- Why should they come?

Aspect-Strengthening Exercises

Checklist for the Gathering at Hand

- Have I (internally and externally) sincerely invited each person to engage?
- Have I envisioned/imagined how I will welcome participants when they arrive?
- Am I prepared to follow through with my sincerity throughout the gathering?

EXERCISE 1: NAMING

An elegant yet powerful exercise to create alignment and extend an effective invitation that expresses hospitality, generosity, and conviction in advance of any meeting is surprisingly simple.

The principle: *When we hold people in our most positive thoughts, it creates a powerful field that brings them into our intention.*

The practice:

Step 1. Before a gathering, write down the name of each of those who will attend so that you can read them all out loud. Reading names the night before allows you to sleep on them, or you may try it the day of. This process has multiple benefits for our gathering, including the reinforcement of the sincerity of the invitation.

Step 2. Find a quiet place where you are able to concentrate as the names are read (either by the Convener alone or by a team). We envision each person as welcome to the meeting, ready to share his or her valuable gifts. There is something especially honoring to the participants in doing this. It translates into a genuine expression of appreciation as we go forward with the gathering.

EXERCISE 2: CREATING THE WELCOME

Before your next meeting or gathering, create a specific method for how you intend to greet and welcome people into the room or physical space. If you've just read the names of those invited, imagine greeting them, modeling the clear expectation of presence, engagement, and participation.

Journaling Questions

Recall a time when you extended an invitation in your professional life. What was at the heart of it, and what was the compelling reason for the invitee to attend?

1. Were your intention and the construction of the invitation aligned with each other and in integrity with who you are?
2. If not, what could you have done differently?
3. When, if ever, has fear of rejection gotten in the way of your extending an invitation? Consider what might have been lost as a result.

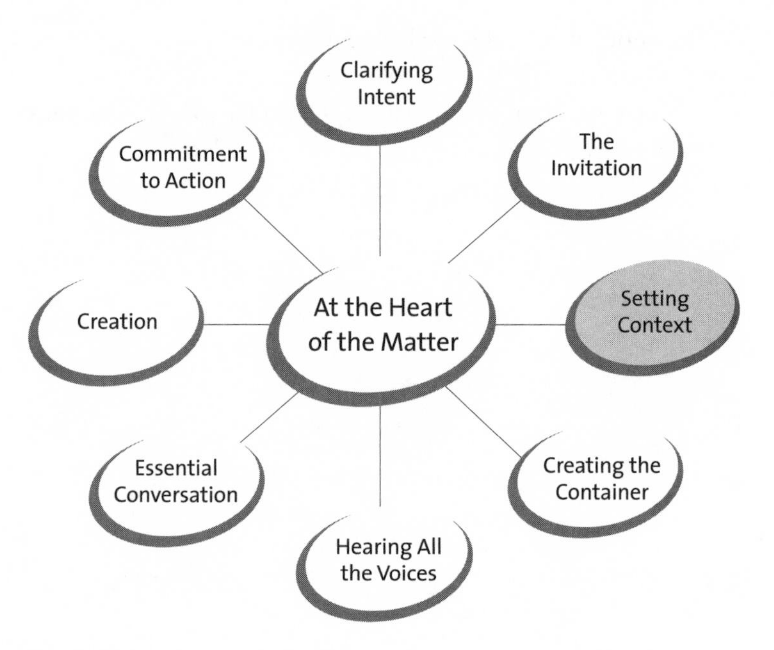
Clarifying Intent
The Invitation
Setting Context
Creating the Container
Hearing All the Voices
Essential Conversation
Creation
Commitment to Action
At the Heart of the Matter

4. SETTING CONTEXT

Communicating the form, function, and purpose of our engagement

WHY SET CONTEXT?

When we optimally prepare people for the form, function, and purpose of our gathering, they will be present in a way that greatly improves the chances of our purpose being actualized. Authentic engagement is more likely when we all have the same historical context or history of "how we've gotten to where we are."

> ALL SCIENCE *is experiential; but all experience must be related back to, and derives its validity from, the conditions and context of consciousness in which it arises, i.e., the totality of our nature.*
>
> —*Wilhelm Dilthey*[1]

When we assume too much about what others know, the result can be confusion and lack of purpose. We can greatly improve the chances of all participants' understanding the context of our gathering if we practice articulating it by writing it down and checking it out ourselves or with others.

WHAT'S THIS GATHERING ABOUT?

Having determined our purpose and clear intent, and offered a genuine, sincere invitation, we're now fully invested in our engagement. When we've done our inner homework, we embody a noticeable quality of confidence and inner commitment. We now need to tell everyone what this gathering is all about.

If the context of our meeting is to make decisions about an organization's future, our participants will naturally put themselves in a state of mind, heart, and spirit required for that type of meeting. That state may be quite different than it would be if the purpose of the gathering were to focus on reporting the progress of an ongoing project or to plan a birthday celebration.

CHALLENGE

Assumption

The Challenge we face and address in this Aspect is *Assumption*. When we assume that others already know what we know, we begin to skip explanations and put the purpose for our gathering squarely into the unknown. To move through this challenge, we need to accurately communicate, verbally or visually, the purpose of our gathering without ambiguity.

> *Don't establish the*
> *boundaries*
> *first*
> *the squares, triangles,*
> *boxes*
> *of preconceived*
> *possibility,*
> *and then*
> *pour*
> *life into them, trimming*
> *off left-over potential;*
> *let centers*
> *proliferate*
> *from*
> *self-justifying motions!*
>
> —A. R. Ammons[2]

ASSUME AND DOOM

We've all arrived at a meeting or conversation with someone only to realize early in the session that we didn't get "the memo" or that the communication we did get was not clear. Once things get started, we find ourselves having to guess, reframe, or give up. Blank stares and deafening silence may be the telltale signs. No matter how important, or minor, the meeting's topic—it is risky and can be time wasting to assume that the purpose, meaning, and needed framing have been fully absorbed and understood by everyone in advance.

PRINCIPLE

The clear articulation of purpose and intent allows the highest potential for the actualization of that purpose.

(Tattoo this principle on your brain.)

Setting Context is the Aspect in which we bring form and function together with purpose and meaning in a clearly articulated statement that informs everyone why we are gathering. When compelling intent is matched with clearly articulated form (external invitation and stated context), we've prepared the ground for the participants to create something new and unique. Imagine your role as articulator and catalyst for this distinct possibility.

Behind each well-conceived invitation is the challenge to live up to its promise.

Imagine the situation described earlier, but this time the Convener opens the meeting or conversation by restating the purpose and intent as articulated in the *Invitation* (and agenda), along with the desired goals and outcomes. We then have an opportunity to be united in purpose and prepared to offer the gift that is called for. Taking time at the outset of any gathering to seek clarity pays off in this fast-paced world where multitasking rules the day and distraction is a threat to understanding.

If we are to realize the highest potential of the gathering, we need to make it possible for everyone to be working on all cylinders. Clearly *Setting Context* harnesses not only the brain, but also the heart and spirit of the convened. Being transparent about our agenda, about the potential for our discourse and our intent, goes a long way toward creating the kind of trust that makes authentic engagement, the precursor to the success of our gathering, possible.

ESSENTIAL QUESTIONS

What is this gathering about?

What do the participants need to know to show up ready to fully participate?

What is our individual and collective purpose for this engagement, and for the sake of what do we do this work?

These Essential Questions require that we take the time, once again, to reflect deeply in order to articulate the answers with precision and grace. Our commitment must be to offer participants as clear and compelling a vision, based on the value and potential for our time together, as we possibly can. When we extend the *Invitation,* we are saying, "You matter." When we are *Setting Context,* we are saying, "What we are to do together matters." The journaling questions at the end of the chapter will help you to imagine and practice doing this for a potential gathering.

MAKING IT REAL

At our staff meetings—or any meeting, for that matter—the first thing we do (after a hearty welcome, of course) as Conveners is to *set the context* for our time together so that all of the participants hear and understand why they have been invited and what the gathering is *for* and *about*. The participants can then choose to place themselves in the best state of *mind, heart,* and *being* to engage in this particular context. This articulation also allows the rational mind (the part of us that is alert for stability and security) to feel safe enough to enter into the unknown part of our gathering—the relationship with others—to create something new.

One helpful practice for accurate context setting is to write down the desired purpose for the gathering in no more than three sentences and then read it out loud either alone or to a partner. Listen for clarity. If there is a way in which the context could be misunderstood, or is misinterpreted by a partner, we make revisions until it seems as clear as possible.

Here's a variation on the same theme: Write down or record yourself (audio or video) explaining the context (reason) for a meeting or gathering. Is it clear? Check it out by having someone else listen, view, read. Notice what might be missing or where misunderstandings might appear.

This small thing, done thoughtfully, can prime our meeting or gathering for great success. Done badly or not at all, it greatly reduces the potential for actualizing our purpose.

HISTORICAL CONTEXT SETTING, OR THE GENESIS STORY

While a clear statement of purpose, or agenda, may be sufficient for some gatherings, others require further context—especially when participants do not have relevant shared historical knowledge. We call this kind of context setting the *genesis story*. It is important to know the origins and history of the people, place, and context of our gathering so that the shared knowledge of this story connects us to each other. As Conveners, we remember that people want to know how they fit into a situation. Telling and retelling the genesis story of how we all came to be at this gathering can powerfully and efficiently achieve this connection.

We've hosted Thought Leader Gatherings each month for the past 12 years. Every session, we briefly tell the genesis story of how we began—the founding premise, and who has been involved, and why. We make the connection between our origins, why we are here today, and what we will do. We describe the thread that has bound us together all these years. This is *Setting Context* that brings people into what is commonly known as the culture of the community or organization, and also invites new people to imagine themselves as part of the whole, or continuum.

Effectively executing *Setting Context* before a meeting or gathering enables participants to show up in the best frame of mind to actualize the purpose. Effectively communicating *Setting Context* at the start of the gathering reinforces this frame and begins to connect the group. When people understand that their personal success is interdependent with that of the group and vice versa, they have the opportunity to move forward to the next level of trust, respect, and authentic engagement.

THE RISK OF NOT *SETTING CONTEXT*

We've addressed the virtues of clear communication and how purpose and intent in alignment with fully articulated context sets the stage for the next Aspect on the Convening Wheel, *Creating the Container*. What happens if the context is not set or the setting is done poorly? What are the risks? In most cases, when people don't see themselves in a connected movement toward a goal or outcome together, there is hesitation, doubt, and, potentially, withholding of vital energy—or even rejection.

Indications of resistance to moving forward include multitasking, background talking, palpable levels of energetic stress in the room, and blank stares. Optimally, people feel safe enough to stand and be vocally challenging if there are questions to be asked or comments to be made. It's important not to feel or act annoyed or threatened, but rather to welcome discourse. At least now we have something concrete to work with. All of these are just opportunities to clarify. Once these obstacles are seen, we take the opportunity to reset.

What if it's clear that we don't have agreement for going forward after *Setting Context*? Take a quick "time in" to recalibrate the purpose and intent of the meeting; then reframe the context, if necessary. Good facilitation skills may come in handy now. Sense, listen, and ask. Well-placed questions are an effective tool in this recalibration. Before moving on, we may ask, "Does the context of this meeting make sense to you?" "Are there any questions before we move on?" "Would someone like to mirror back to me what I've just said?" or "What have you heard is the context of this meeting?"

Once again, we state our intent and purpose clearly, and ask for reflections or feedback. As we practice our convening, we become more tuned in to the nuances and subtleties of the mood, body language, and what we call "people sense" in the room. Then, when resistance is experienced within the group, we are ready and grounded in our response.

TRANSITIONS

Another way to recalibrate and bring the group into a thoughtful presence is to utilize a Transition Exercise. Transitions are an important and often-neglected aspect of any gathering. Whether at the beginning, as people settle into their chairs, or with a change from process to process, transitions are "the spaces in-between" and another opportunity to keep participants present to themselves.

Like cleansing the palate between courses, a Transition Exercise, whether it is a poem, a meditation, a visualization, stretching of arms or legs, or just a brief breathing exercise, helps people to re-center and recalibrate, to be fully present for what comes next.

For the Convener to be aware and fully present to each transition is a constant practice. There are many ways to create this awareness.

Pay attention to when topics change or the group is to move on to a different part of the agenda. Keeping a flow that is consistent with the understood context of our gathering is important. Exercise 2 at the end of the chapter offers an example of a Transition Exercise that is used consistently in Heartland gatherings and meetings.

Where We Are on the Convening Wheel

1. *At the Heart of the Matter*—We have explored who we are and how we will be in relationship with others.
2. *Clarifying Intent*—We have identified an intention consistent with *At the Heart of the Matter* that has substance and is acted upon.
3. *The Invitation*—We have extended a sincere invitation with genuine hospitality, generosity, and conviction.
4. *Setting Context*—We have clearly communicated the form, function, and purpose of our gathering.

Setting Context has prepared the minds, hearts, and spirit of the Convener and participants for what will come later in the engagement. Now we move on to prepare the external and internal boundaries and space of our engagement by *Creating the Container.*

Things to Remember

Challenge: *Assumption*

Principle: *Clear articulation of purpose and intent allows the highest potential for the actualization of that purpose.*

Essential Questions:

- What is this gathering about?
- What do the participants need to know to show up and fully participate?
- What is our individual and collective purpose for this engagement, and for the sake of what do we do this work?

Aspect-Strengthening Exercises

Checklist for the Gathering at Hand

- Have I clearly articulated to everyone the form, function, and purpose of this gathering?
- Have I verified the clarity of my communication with at least one other person?

EXERCISE 1: DEVELOPING THE CONTEXT "MUSCLE"

Write it!

Find a quiet time and place to write for at least 20 minutes. Write down the context (reason, form, and function) for a specific meeting or gathering. Go through the thought process just as you would want someone to articulate the context of the gathering to you.

Make sure you have answered the following questions:

- What is the genesis story of this engagement?
- What is this gathering about?
- What do the participants need to know to show up and fully participate?
- What is our individual and collective purpose for this engagement, and for the sake of what do we do this work?
- Who will we be together?
- What will a successful meeting look like?

Speak it!

Speak it out loud to yourself, or, better yet, to another or into an audio/video recorder. The point here is to practice out loud just the way others will hear you. It's not enough to think it—speak it.

Repeat it!

Ask for honest reflection from others. Adapt, revise, and modify based on what you hear. Same with audio/video. It is hard to hear and see yourself, however, it's what others will see and hear; why not know how others will experience you?

EXERCISE 2: TRANSITIONS

The following is a Transition Exercise you may wish to consider using in your engagements. We use this to prepare for a meeting, or to pause and recalibrate during a meeting. We may choose to introduce it to the group at the meeting outset or during a time of transition during the meeting. Its beauty is in its efficiency: normally we allow one to three minutes to complete; however, it can be modified to less than 30 seconds with good results.

Transition Exercise[3]

1. Find a comfortable place to sit with your feet on the floor and your hands free if possible.
2. If you're comfortable to do so, close your eyes and notice your breathing. Otherwise, just soften your gaze, looking forward at a fixed object.
3. Shift your focus away from your mind to the area around your heart.
4. Imagine yourself breathing through your heart. It may help to put your hand on your heart.
5. Keep your focus there for 10 seconds or more.
6. Now, recall a time in which you felt appreciation or gratitude for someone or something, and attempt to reexperience it.
7. Notice the feeling.
8. When you're ready, open your eyes or refocus your gaze to be present.

Journaling Questions

Imagine a meeting or gathering you may have in the future.

1. How would you articulate the form, function, purpose, and desired outcomes for your engagement?
2. How would your articulation be received?
3. How would it affect the nature of the engagement?
4. What difference can you imagine between doing this and not setting context—or giving it less attention?

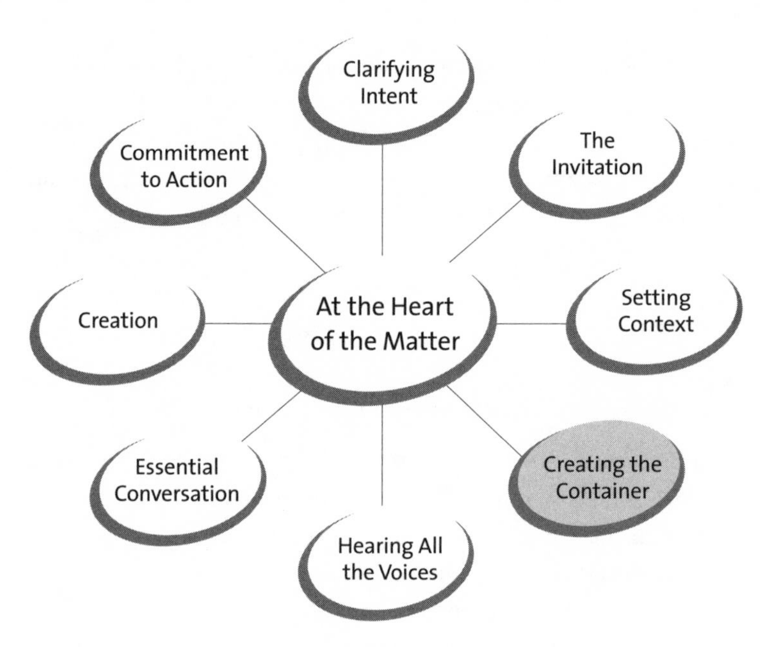
Clarifying Intent
The Invitation
Setting Context
Creating the Container
Hearing All the Voices
Essential Conversation
Creation
Commitment to Action
At the Heart of the Matter

5. CREATING THE CONTAINER

Creating the physical and energetic field within which we meet

WHY A CONTAINER?

Creating the Container is about providing an environment for our gathering that is enlivened, has boundaries, and is safe. When the participants of our gathering feel honored as human beings and encircled in safety, authentic engagement can emerge. In order to achieve this, we pay attention to the space, both energetic and physical, in which we will be "held" during the duration of the meeting.

It is important that we prepare both of these spaces, or *fields*, so that we have an inner and an outer container to hold the gathering.

The inner, or energetic, container provides security and safety so that those within may freely express themselves. The outer, or physical, container reminds us of our humanity and aliveness, and encourages connection.

Selection of venue, size, shape, and what we bring to it are all part of preparing the outer container. This can be done in a physical space or virtually (see "The Virtual Container," below). Our meeting space will also be defined by the seating pattern, whether rows, theater style, or circle.

In addition to the physical space, the inner, or energetic, container is designed and prepared with an eye to safety within strong boundaries. This is achieved by having *terms of engagement,* or the protocols and agreements that will be observed for the gathering. The Convener may define these and ask for agreement from all participants. Important protocols and agreements include confidentiality, marking of time, who may speak and when, and how we are to acknowledge or speak to each other.

CHALLENGE

Reluctance to impose our will on others

Strong boundaries, the very nature of a container, established by our protocols and agreements, are essential for safety to be present within the group, and for the emergence of authentic engagement.

The challenge of this Aspect of convening is, ironically, our reluctance to impose our will on others.

This can be a tough and elusive challenge for many people who have been trained or conditioned to be flexible and free-wheeling in social interactions and who don't wish to be perceived as pushy, authoritarian, or rigid. The flip side of not wishing to impose our will is equally challenging. The "my way or the highway" manager may get compliance, but not necessarily respect and an environment of safety when mandating command-and-control rules and regulations.

The expression of our inner authority and confidence as a Convener is crucial, as is our willingness to step forward, and to name and ask for agreement to the terms of engagement.

Without clearly stated agreements and protocols up front, everyone may be left to define his or her own unstated boundaries and conditions for participation, which runs the high risk of dissipating the group's energy. It then takes energy for each of us to create and hold our own terms of engagement because we don't know what might be acceptable to the others in the room that might violate our boundaries. Our sense of safety is compromised in an anything-goes environment, and it becomes difficult to engage authentically.

In addition to the courage needed to create the inner container, it takes courage to create the outer container. Without a sense of aliveness in the environment, the participants will be less likely to sense their connection to one another. Deliberately enlivening the environment with beauty and an optimal seating arrangement will go far in bringing needed group cohesion.

PRINCIPLE

Clear and accepted boundaries integrated with an enlivened environment allow safety and openness.

If we expect the participants of any gathering to be authentically engaged, open, honest, and perhaps vulnerable, as well as to feel connected to one another, the Convener's role is to be vitally aware of and attentive to the energetic boundaries and physical conditions of the gathering—simultaneously.

When we speak of "holding the people," a large part of what we are referring to is this attentiveness to the inner and outer containers. Our attention to these boundaries and conditions is a precious gift to the participants of our gathering, creating the potential for their wholehearted openness.

ESSENTIAL QUESTIONS

What is needed for the participants to feel safe in this gathering?

What will enliven the environment?

What protocols and agreements must be present?

We ask ourselves these questions so that we will be prepared to create the container for our engagement when the time comes. We return to the questions over and over as we design the space for our gathering and as we think about what the agreements and protocols will be.

Our surroundings play a vital role, so we consider carefully where we will meet. Whatever space we choose, we ask ourselves how we will enliven the environment for optimal connection.

We might find that each gathering we convene requires the same or similar terms of engagement, or we may find that the participants of certain engagements require very specific or customized agreements and protocols in order to feel safe. Part of our work here will be to keep our attention on what is needed for the particular group that is gathering.

MAKING IT REAL

The outer and inner containers for our gathering require thoughtful consideration.

OUTER CONTAINER

The physical container is the location or place in which we meet. When the environment is alive and has beauty, the space itself feels inviting and welcoming. An office space or conference room with windows; a charming restaurant; a sidewalk café; or a public space with exposure to a pretty view, art, living plants, and beauty can be perfect for some types of gatherings. Sometimes, though, we don't have the luxury of choosing where we will meet or gather. As Conveners, we still ask ourselves how best to enliven the environment we will be in to honor the participants as living human beings.

In places prepared with thoughtfulness, we are more likely to feel a stronger human connection. To bring this aliveness to the environment, we prepare the room or space so that there is something of nature, art, and/or beauty present. A vase of flowers in the center of the room, art, an engaging view of the outdoors, and an arrangement of natural objects are all things we use to our advantage to create a living environment.

OUR MEETING PLACES MATTER. Often we are faced with meeting spaces that are angular, sharp-edged, and devoid of natural lighting, windows, and art. Sometimes little to no attention has been given to bringing the full human experience to our workplaces or other social institutions. It often seems odd to hear music or experience beauty outside of the occasional celebration in our offices.

> CARE INSPIRES *and gently reassures us. Lending us a feeling of security and support, it reinforces our connection with others. Not only is it one of the best things we can do for our health, but it feels good—whether we're giving or receiving it.*
>
> —*Doc Childre and Howard Martin*[1]

We spend much, if not most, of our work lives indoors, engaged in our individual passions and labors either alone or with others. Do we give the same care and attention to our work and meeting spaces as we may to our homes and other living situations? Do we treat them with the same care and friendship as we do our favorite places? Do our meeting spaces bring us to life or bring us down?

The spaces designated for us to meet are often no more than a nondescript cube in which we're expected to carry out the most inspired work of the day. The room may include chairs and tables; media to service our communication needs; bright lights; spare walls; and—at best—a few windows, subdued art, and perhaps a potted plant. This is what we have come to expect of our meeting spaces.

A primary rationale for our lack of attention to our outer container is the concern about *losing control* over our surroundings. It goes something like this: if we bring too much of our personal selves (human qualities)—beauty, heart, compassion, creativity, and so on—into our meetings, we'll lose our clearheaded objectivity and focus that drive results. The distrust is that, unless we control the environment with little to no outside stimuli, people will goof off and ultimately be unproductive.

If we don't create venues and spaces that allow for authentic engagement to emerge, then we'll pay for it in the long run when *committed action* is called for from the people. Trust and respect are directly proportionate to the level of belonging and interdependence that people feel in their relationship to one another. Without an experience of authentic connectivity, lasting commitment and accountability to one another and the task at hand is not likely.

We often create a circular seating arrangement when we convene at Heartland because it induces a collegial feel, and everyone can see and be seen by everyone else. This configuration also facilitates authentic engagement among the participants. It takes some courage to set the room in a way that may be unexpected or considered frivolous, but we continue to create the environment that seems the most conducive to our objective of bringing authentic engagement to the group.

Surroundings that allow us to feel secure and give us a sense of belonging tend to make us less apprehensive and stressful. When we feel safe and taken care of in our outer world, our inner world follows suit. We have a better chance of approaching our engagement as whole and healthy people to the degree that we experience security and connectivity to our surroundings and our colleagues, family, or friends.

PRACTICAL MATTERS IN CREATING THE OUTER CONTAINER. The possible configurations in which we design our meetings and gatherings are limitless. Let's begin by considering our intent, the content, and outcomes. Think of your meeting space as a blank canvas, and that you are building on its assets rather than liabilities.

Consider how to maximize presence, connectivity, understanding, and action. These are the foundational objectives for any engagement.

> ***Presence.*** We've laid the groundwork for everyone to be present through setting context and accepted agreements for our engagement. Now, how do we play on the physical design of the meeting space to

maximize the full presence of everyone throughout the session?

Connectivity. What design forms allow for high levels of essential interaction among the participants—interaction that stimulates learning, retention, creativity, and ultimately a commitment to action?

Understanding. Access to knowledge and information is not a requirement for absorption and understanding. When we provide environments where presence and connectivity are valued, the potential for the assimilation of information and knowledge into useful understanding is greatly enhanced. Understanding is the gateway to wisdom.

Action. Has our space been designed to take advantage of the opportunities to bring our creativity to full flower through action?

Action may be defined in many ways, from meaningful conversation to specific outcomes. In *The Answer to How Is Yes: Acting on What Matters,* Peter Block tells us that conversation may be the ultimate action step.[2]

Start slowly and build. We are creatures of our own traditions and rituals. Make small design changes and build from there.

In the box below is a discussion of some often-overlooked issues to consider when designing the physical space of a meeting or gathering. Think about these suggestions and tips as generalized principles you may apply to your own setting with the objective of having an enlivened environment, and proceed from that perspective.

THE SPACE

Take an inventory of the architecture, design, and amenities of the space in which you are working. What do you have to work with? Look at everything as a tool in your tool kit. Use cultural icons whenever possible, familiar images, perhaps company logos or other symbols.

Windows/lighting. The ability to see the world outside of the meeting room often changes the mood of the participants. For instance, at a recent meeting where people could see natural beauty outside, many commented that the beautiful view was calming and satisfying, leading to a greater capacity to participate.

If your space does not have natural lighting, can you bring in floor lighting to soften the glare of overhead lights?

Walls. As an interior designer, what do you have to work with? Artwork? Textiles or tapestry? Even flip-chart paper or quotes on squares can break up broad expanses to create more interesting spaces in which to spend time.

Doors. Where are they in relation to the meeting space? Doors offer opportunity and surprise. Be aware of and seek to control where and how people enter and exit the meeting, if possible. A good configuration will enable late-arriving participants to be less disruptive and lessens the chance that passersby will be inadvertently distracting.

Media. Many of our gatherings employ all sorts of media, from screened presentations to audio surround and personal devices of every shape and size. The rule here is to know when they are useful or not, and then have clear, agreed-upon protocols for when and how they are used. In this age of cell phones, iPods, BlackBerrys, and other ubiquitous personal devices, clearly indicate what is expected to be off, silent, or on. Otherwise, the room could become a hijacked media ping-pong match.

Tables and chairs. When possible, rearrange and configure furniture to your purpose.

- Know that whoever is standing is in charge and has the stage.
- Know that tables are great for storing and holding stuff, but not necessarily beneficial for engendering meaningful discourse.
- Know that rows of chairs, theater style, allow people to hide and make it harder to keep their attention.
- Know that most chairs are uncomfortable, and 40 minutes in one sitting is about all that people can take.
- Know that you have the right and permission to shift the energy by playing musical chairs when the time is right, perhaps after a break.

Make sure that your seating arrangement takes these things into consideration. We think that having everyone seated in an open circle is the best configuration for most of our gatherings, but other configurations may be optimal for certain types of gatherings (see below).

CIRCLES, SQUARES, AND ROWS

How we meet defines the conversation. Although there are varied contexts for our meetings, the circle, square, and row seem to be the forms in which we meet the most. So let's look at what is best for what type of gathering.

Squares. Our most familiar form of gathering for meetings is in geometric configurations around tables. We also tend to meet around tables in more informal settings, such as at coffeehouses and restaurants. The table-and-chairs format is well suited for cognitive and intellectual exchanges of data and information. We are able to cohabitate with media, food, and other meeting props as we engage. These formats tend to be more formal, sacrificing the full body intimacy of the circle for the purpose of more utilitarian exchanges. Utility and the transaction of ideas, information, and concepts are its strengths.

Rows. Theater-style meetings are best used for clear and direct presentations, whatever their content. The row configuration is best used for absorption and learning in an efficient use of space where all *consumers* are able to experience the same material at the same time, and there is no wish for them to participate any further (except possibly in limited ways, such as a question-and-answer segment).

The circle. The most ancient "technology" for human gatherings most likely started around the campfire and continues today as the most effective form of creating presence and connectivity. The circle creates equality and peerage among those present, even in a hierarchical environment. As a practical matter, we use a single-circle seating configuration for our gatherings typically of groups of under 75 people, without microphones. We have found that concentric circles for larger-scale assemblages are effective in achieving intimacy as well. The practical advantages of circle seating are as follows:

- Everyone can see and hear one another. Imagine meetings where all can see and hear one another. There is no hiding out in the circle. Without tables, there is a presence and a demand for attention to one another that no other meeting form affords.
- It induces a nonhierarchical structure in which sharing at a more engaged level is accepted and invited.
- Circles provide recognition (seeing) of the whole community and are adaptable to smaller breakout groupings for more intimate conversations.
- Circles have been used successfully in community and faith-based venues, and more recently have been introduced into business settings because they allow participants to get to the heart of the matter more quickly than do other meeting forms.

Note the United Nations and various round-table discussion groups as examples of collegial environments using the circle.

Changing the physical space takes courage. People will react. Take a deep breath, knowing that you are bringing your gift to the group.

THE BEST "BEST IN THE WEST"

As one of the senior organizational development (OD) planners for the upcoming Best in the West Conference, an event held every year by the San Francisco Bay Area OD Network Conference attendees, I had an inspiration! Rather than bemoaning the uninspiring and flat opening of previous conferences, we decided to use the structure and design elements of the Art of Convening.

I seized the opportunity to design an opening that reflected the spirit of our OD practices and create real community among us. I spoke with the keynoter, the conference chairs, and the board chair to clarify the intent and ensure that we were all aligned. I enlisted two to three close colleagues to assist and support the process.

On the day of the event, as emcee, after setting the context for the conference, I invited participants to join me in the circle—and a big circle it was, in a cavernous auditorium with three circles of chairs to accommodate 170 people. There was a beautiful centerpiece of purple and white irises on a purple and white cloth. What a contrast to the year before! I asked permission to convene this inspiring and exciting group vibrating with energy. I then invited everyone to take a deep breath and, in a moment of silence, to become present from their travels to the conference, and to reflect on their intent for the day . . . learning new skills, networking and meeting new colleagues, presenting or learning new ideas. I reviewed the agenda for the opening session, which included hearing our speaker, taking a short break in the middle of the presentation to share the implications with a partner, and a closing reflection. After I reviewed the rationale and the ancient history of the circle, the value of seeing each other and hearing all our voices, and how we were creating community, I described the concept and purpose of "stringing the beads," and we began to hear all the voices of those present in the room.

These were not new structure or design elements for OD practitioners, but it was new to bring these elements to the opening session of the conference in such a large group. Because of predetermined schedules, there was not as much time as I would have liked to create this opening community event. But despite the time constraints, it worked! Many attendees talked about the welcome sense of openness, the spirit of sharing, and the feeling of community that carried through the day. Perhaps next year will bring a more flexible schedule.

—By Bev Scott[3]

THE INNER CONTAINER

The energetic field or inner container for our gathering refers to the energy or chemistry created and sensed within the people attending. This field is created with the terms of engagement, or the agreements and protocols we hold for our gathering. Protocols and agreements serve as the social norms of our container, allowing people to feel safe enough to share their gifts at a meaningful level. Feeling safe is imperative if we are to bring authentic engagement to the group.

We have a love/hate relationship with structure. When the social form and function is clearly stated and agreed upon, an energy is released that allows the container to be formed. In the absence of clear and requested agreements, there is no freedom within the assembled. Knowing the terms of engagement enables

> SOME THINGS *may seem obvious—such as if you wish to facilitate the emergence of collective wisdom from the center of a group of people, there must first be a container. Without boundaries, without a conscious container, there is no center through which wisdom can emerge. The basic form of container that I work with both literally and figuratively is the circle. The circle is the oldest symbol I am aware of for Oneness or Wholeness.*
>
> —*Pele Rouge Chadima*[4]

the participants to make an informed choice to accept or not. There are ways to elegantly navigate this element.

ASKING FOR AGREEMENT. We've identified *reluctance to impose our will* as the main challenge in *Creating the Container*. Being perceived as authoritarian or rigid can be uncomfortable for many of us. However, establishing boundaries requires us to be neither authoritarian nor rigid. *We simply ask the others for agreement.* Part of this asking, and a way to convey that we are the Convener, is to ask the group for permission to be the Convener.

Since we are the ones calling the meeting and inviting people to attend, we may think it is assumed (see chapter 4) that we are the Convener, but it is important to the common understanding of the gathering going forward that we restate our role as Convener and ask for permission (get buy-in) to assume this role. The participants are likely to experience security in knowing who's in the leadership role.

Once there is a common understanding that we are the Convener, we briefly describe what the Convener will do. For example, the Convener will mark time, will lead transitions, and will open and close the gathering.

Once we are established as the Convener, we state the protocols and terms of engagement for the gathering. There is some flexibility here, but important protocols that are almost always present in our gatherings are confidentiality (what is said here stays here), how we are to acknowledge and respect who has the floor, and when people are expected to listen or to speak.

For large groups or for groups on the phone, an efficient and effective practice is to tell people that their silence signifies agreement. Of course, the participants must then have the ability and freedom to speak up if they don't agree. Another (more time-consuming and messy but perhaps necessary for some groups) way to obtain agreement is to poll each person one by one, asking for "yea or nay" or a show of hands.

UNLOCKING THE CONTAINER

As the women arrived, I could sense an energetic jumble of feelings, including both anticipation and hesitation. My first task, as coach and facilitator, is to create a safe container for our time together.

The stated purpose of our session is to "unlock our passion, potential, and purpose for joyful living." To create the spaciousness for this to occur requires certain structures and protocols that allow for the wisdom and willingness of the group to emerge.

After a brief meet and greet, I rang a small bell and invited the 10 women into the circle. This welcoming space had been prepared with comfortable chairs gathered around a beautifully carved low table, where I had placed both candles and flowers along with several strands of colorful beads. This would serve as the focal point of our *physical container* for our time together.

Creating an *energetic container* conducive to engaging in rich and meaningful conversations was next. I began by enumerating certain agreements and protocols that would provide safety and structure for our gathering. The women were asked to detach from phones and other distractions, to leave their to-do lists behind, and to commit to being fully present. We spoke about the circle and its deeper symbolic meaning, and then discussed the need for absolute confidentiality. When I assured them that no one would be asked to share anything beyond her personal comfort level, I could feel a collective sigh of relief. Finally, I explained the format for respectful listening, sharing, and conversation that we would adhere to, and that it would be my responsibility to "hold the space" and to move things along.

—By Minx Boren[5]

CREATING THE VIRTUAL CONTAINER

Our attention so far in this book has been focused mainly on "in person" engagements. Our multimedia world offers us a much broader range of opportunities to convene in the virtual world, from conference call meetings and webinars to social media network gatherings and other electronically based community environments.

Since 2004, Heartland has pioneered convening in virtual space through our Art of Convening TeleTrainings using telephone and Internet technologies as the gathering and learning platform for teaching the principles and practices of convening.

After six years of practical application with hundreds of classes and thousands of contact hours, we've found that the core principles of the Convening Wheel apply to virtual as well as in-person gatherings. There is no discernable difference between the fundamental ways in which we convene by conference call or in an onsite meeting.

In the story to follow, we'll see how the "virtual container" is a very effective way of *Creating the Container* for a gathering on the phone or in another medium where we are not physically together.

Don't underestimate the power of the human imagination to create the perfect setting in which to meet. With help from the Convener, the participants are able to imagine themselves together in a setting that, while customized to each individual, provides a common area to gather and "see" one another. The following story illustrates how we create a virtual "place" in the campfire around which we meet. Using our imaginations, we're able to place ourselves together in an environment that we can hold as real for the duration of our time together.

As you'll see in the following story, agreements and protocols become essential in the creation of the virtual container.

THE VIRTUAL CAMPFIRE

The Art of Convening TeleTraining group had arrived. Each of 10 participants, from various parts of the country, had dialed in to a two-hour teleconference session by phone. Each was greeted by name with a heartfelt "Welcome" and engaged in lighthearted conversation as the time to start approached. At the scheduled time, Craig, the Convener, said, "Let's begin."

Craig announced the context for the session, with its themes and agenda, and introduced the co-Convener. He then stated the protocols to be observed on the call, requesting that each participant agree or not to the following:

> **"We agree to be fully present.** To call from a quiet place alone and free of distractions, excusing ourselves from all other engagements; we disconnect from e-mail, computers, and electronic media.
>
> **"We agree to confidentiality.** What is said on this call stays within this group. Please don't share with people outside of this group.
>
> **"We agree to identify ourselves.** We will say 'I am' and our name when we begin to speak, and 'I am complete' or some other closing signal when we are finished speaking so that others may know we are not just pausing.
>
> **"We agree to ask for what we need and look for surprises."** Craig continued, "I ask your permission to be the Convener. I'll be marking time and leading the session."
>
> "If you don't agree or have questions about these protocols, please speak up; otherwise, I take your silence to signify your acceptance." He paused for a few seconds in silence. No one spoke.
>
> Acknowledging that they were each in separate spaces and had only the virtual space connecting them, Craig asked the participants to imagine themselves sitting around a campfire. He began, "Imagine the weather is pleasant, the fire is warm and inviting, and we are all seated comfortably, able to see one another around the fire . . ." He continued to set the scene for an intimate group sitting around a campfire, together.

Thus the virtual container was created. As the session proceeded, the participants were held, virtually, in an atmosphere of natural life, beauty, and safety.[6]

AGREEMENTS AND PROTOCOLS CHECKLIST

1. Start on time and end on time. People trust people who are punctual and clear about their time boundaries. Punctuality is a sign of respect and shows that we take each other seriously.
2. Know who is convening, and ask for permission from the assembled for that person to convene, especially if it is a shared or co-led event.
3. An efficient way to ask for permission of any sort from the group is to state, "Your silence signifies agreement. If you have questions or don't agree, please speak up; otherwise, agreement is assumed."
4. Be sensitive to when confidentiality is appropriate, and ask for agreement from everyone when this is the case. Simply say, "Whatever is said here stays within this group. Share your experience but not that of anyone else by name."
5. Humor and not taking ourselves too seriously is always a good idea.
6. Make clear the cultural norms you will be observing, or not. Examples: Prayer at the beginning of a faith group. Acknowledging hierarchical norms during meetings (for example, "In this meeting, we will use first names.").

Where We Are on the Convening Wheel

1. *At the Heart of the Matter*—We have explored who we are and how we will be in relationship with others.
2. *Clarifying Intent*—We have identified an intention consistent with *At the Heart of the Matter* that has substance and is acted upon.
3. *The Invitation*—We have extended a sincere invitation with genuine hospitality, generosity, and conviction.

4. *Setting Context*—We have clearly communicated the form, function, and purpose of our gathering.
5. *Creating the Container*—We have prepared a physical space with beauty and life, and we have agreed on terms of engagement or protocols that bring safety for our time together.

Creating the Container provides us with a safe and conducive space for our engagement to unfold. As the participants settle into this container, we call each to be "present and accounted for" by *Hearing All the Voices*—the next Aspect of the Convening Wheel.

Things to Remember

Challenge: *Reluctance to impose our will on others. Are we willing to step forward to establish the boundaries of the gathering?*

Principle: *Clear and accepted boundaries integrated with an enlivened environment allows for safety and openness.*

Essential Questions:

- What is needed for the participants to feel safe in this gathering?
- What will enliven the environment?
- What protocols and agreements must be present?

Aspect-Strengthening Exercises

Checklist for the Gathering at Hand

- Does the gathering environment feel alive? If not, what can I do to introduce life and beauty?
- Do I know what the terms of engagement will be, and am I prepared to ask for all to agree?

EXERCISE 1: REFLECTING ON BEAUTY

Recall the last time you experienced an expression of beauty in your meetings. What were the psychic, emotional, and physical impacts on the people, and the outcomes?

- Pick out one or two elements that were meaningful to you, to begin to create a standard for future engagements.

- Experiment with them to create a baseline form for your engagements.

EXERCISE 2: PICTURING

Picturing an upcoming meeting, create a list of new ways to bring beauty and aliveness, and to activate the space.

- Experiment with ways to bring a room or environment alive with nature (flowers/plants), art, light, sound, temperature, scent, and/or view.
- Is there a fresh way of envisioning the room and its contents, and how participants will interact with one another?
- When you walk into a room, notice and familiarize yourself with the room—windows, doors, other objects, and furniture. Touch each place where a person might sit, and imagine what it would be like to sit there.

Journaling Questions

- In designing physical spaces for human interaction, what considerations would you make for bringing aliveness to the engagement? List some specific examples.
- In designing an engagement to hold a safe field for the people involved, what agreement and protocols would you use? List specific examples.

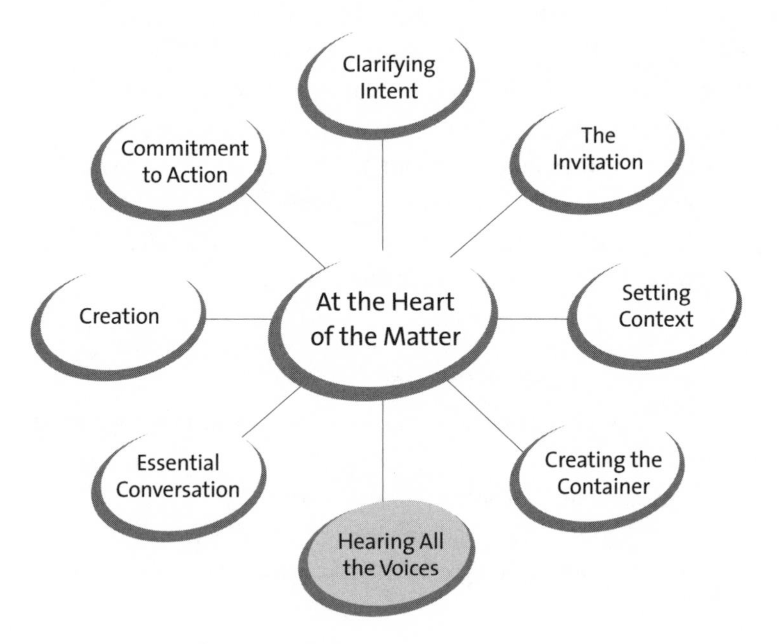
Clarifying Intent
The Invitation
Setting Context
Creating the Container
Hearing All the Voices
Essential Conversation
Creation
Commitment to Action
At the Heart of the Matter

6. HEARING ALL THE VOICES

When each person speaks, is heard, and is present and accounted for

EACH VOICE IS NEEDED AND WANTED

Our container has been created; now is the time to invite each person to say something. *Hearing All the Voices* is the time in our gathering when each person is asked to speak, is heard, and is perceived by everyone as "present and accounted for." It is an imperative Aspect of the Convening Wheel that may make or break our ability to enter into authentic engagement and continue into *Essential Conversation*, the next Aspect on the Convening Wheel.

The art of listening as well as hearing is at play now. The often-delicate environment may be compromised by impatience or judgment. We address this by slowing down the conversation and by inviting all participants to truly suspend judgment of others.

Hearing All the Voices is when we begin to experience the emergence of a wholeness in the gathering. With the coalescence of *intent within a safe container* and *hearing from each person*, a more whole picture begins to emerge. As each person speaks and is heard, people become more present and accounted for to the group. This is the beginning of what we call "listening one another into being."

Our mutual generosity, through speaking and listening, is needed to generate authentic engagement in the group. Generosity is most likely to occur when we are accepted and valued.

CHALLENGE

Impatience and judgment

The challenges we most often encounter in this Aspect of the Wheel are impatience and judgment. Frequently the desire to "get on with it" will threaten to derail this Aspect. We may want to skip this step altogether or skip some of the voices for a variety of reasons, including (but by no means exclusive to) the following:

- It would take too much time.
- People may not have anything important to say.
- We sense that some may not wish to speak or may feel nervous or threatened by the requirement to speak.

We face these challenges by slowing down. Paradoxically, we slow down the mind to overcome the inertia that feeds our impatience. When we slow down the inquiry to the group, the *silence between the notes creates music*. We allow there to be pauses between the speakers, creating the space for individual and collective genius to emerge and be heard.

If we find ourselves, in any way, judging the participants, or the participants are judging each other, there is no quicker way to shut down the energy of the group, rendering the container unsafe. Remembering the lessons learned from *Clarifying Intent* about noticing involuntary communications, it behooves us to be aware of, and suspend, our own judgments, modeling the behaviors that give permission for others to suspend their own. When we do so, we prevent the subtle transmission of those judgments, allowing full, fearless participation by all.

THE RETREAT

There had been a history of tension between the doctors and administrators at the annual four-day retreat for the leadership of a large health-care organization. The doctors often viewed administrators as uncaring "pencil pushers." The administrators often viewed the doctors as "only in it for the money," ignorant of what it took to operate as a viable business. This tension was not openly acknowledged but would often show up as resistance when it was time to make a decision or get something done.

Carol, a Convener, was a senior director in the organization. She persuaded the planning team to start the retreat that year with a large circle where everyone could "check in" (her culturally accepted term for *Hearing All the Voices*). Many of the participants were skeptical. Carol had earned enough respect for her competence and expertise in leading meetings that they were willing to go along with what she wanted, but most doubted that it would make a difference.

Carol had prepared for the retreat by doing her own internal work. She was confident in her purpose for being there at that time. She knew her intention to bring authenticity and cohesion to these leaders, and she had sincerely and warmly invited and welcomed each as the participants arrived that first day. She also thought deeply about a question that would tap the commonality of the group and require some thoughtful reflection.

When all were seated in a circle and it was time to check in, Carol asked that those present, one at a time, say their name, their title, and a couple of sentences about why they chose to be in the health-care field. She asked that they keep their remarks short, from the heart, and that they listen attentively to each other. The responses were all very passionate:

> "I think of it as an honor to heal the sick."
>
> "I want to be part of preserving and improving human life."
>
> "Medicine is fascinating, but really I want to serve as a healer."
>
> "I wanted to choose a business that made a real difference in people's lives."
>
> "I have a passion for caring for the ill."

Those in the circle, both doctors and administrators, were all saying the same things. Judgment seemed to melt. An Arc of Recognition took place, from each to the others, that brought the group together as a whole (see chapter 7).

Later in the retreat, Carol reported that several "breakthroughs" had been made. Participants were able to say things to each other that they hadn't before. Many of the participants later told her that the circle check-in had made the difference in enabling all of the factions to see each other as human beings, similar to themselves—and that was what enabled them to dig deeper, reveal themselves authentically, and accomplish more.[1]

PRINCIPLE

Each voice is needed to reveal the authentic wisdom in our engagement.

We often refer to this principle as *letting go and letting come.*[2] We let go of our preconceptions of who the others are in the gathering, and we let come the truth, quality, and essence of each. We suspend judgment (certainty) so that we are open to the possibilities of others.

We must know, internally, that we, and all the others who are here, belong here. Each is needed and is here to contribute to the potential wisdom and creativity that we want in order to allow for the best possible outcome. There are no mistakes or outsiders in the universe, or in our gathering.

When we acknowledge that each voice is needed, we recognize that we are gathering the parts of something, just as a gardener gathers tools, seeds, and soil in the creation of a garden. As in a garden, where these necessary elements come together, it is so in our gatherings: every person contributes by coming together to create something new. We orchestrate the opportunity for each individual to participate, producing a whole that is greater than the sum of its parts. When all of the voices are heard, everyone sees and is seen by one another. Authentic engagement has begun, and an organic whole begins to emerge.

This is where the phenomenon of *listening one another into being* takes place. When the groundwork is laid by speaking and hearing others speak, people energetically experience being an integral part of the group and have a stake in a successful outcome. The assumption of those gathered tends to shift to *we're all in this together.*

ESSENTIAL QUESTIONS

Who are we, and what have we come to say and do together?

How will we hear all the voices at this gathering?

What methods and practices will allow for the full expression of all participants?

By considering these Essential Questions, we begin *Hearing All the Voices*. Our inner work, *At the Heart of the Matter*, and our clear intention for this gathering will help determine the way we bring each person to speak. The consideration of these questions in our preparation prior to the gathering gives us a logical thought process to work with. There are many dialogic and conversational methods at our disposal for stimulating and engaging the "hearing." We have included one of the most powerful practices in this chapter and in "Arrows for Your Quiver," at the back of the book.

The anxiety that participants may experience when asked to speak can be lessened considerably by properly attending to the Aspects of the Convening Wheel leading up to *Hearing All the Voices*.

If we have done the required work to get *At the Heart of the Matter,* have *clarified intent,* have extended a truly sincere *Invitation,* have followed up with a clear *setting of context,* and, finally, have *created the container* of aliveness and safety for our gathering, then we will have done our part to encourage authentic engagement and set the stage for *Hearing All the Voices*.

MAKING IT REAL

Courage is needed to *hear all the voices*. Don't let embarrassment, impatience, or timidity get in the way. In the absence of *Hearing All the Voices*, the probability is much greater that people will not be present to one another or the meeting in a way that allows for authentic engagement. Our goal is to maximize the genuine presence of each person in the room: physically, emotionally, mentally, and spiritually. If we don't do this, people may not be present in the following ways:

> DEEP LISTENING *is miraculous for both listener and speaker. When someone receives us with open-hearted, non-judging, intensely interested listening, our spirits expand.*
>
> —*Sue Patton Thoele*[3]

Physically. People may turn away, look somewhere else, or leave.

Emotionally. Fear, anger, sadness, or feelings of embarrassment may prevent true, courageous presence.

Mentally. Thoughts of distrust, criticism, or perceived wrongdoing may prevent people from being mentally present.

Spiritually. People may unconsciously resist contributing their presence to the whole.

DEEP LISTENING

Hearing All the Voices is the beginning of the sense of community that is necessary for our gathering to produce authentic engagement and the best possible outcome. It is the mix within which we will lay the seeds of creativity and innovation.

Our desire during this Aspect is to hear from a place of deep listening. We prepare for this by asking all participants to *listen and speak from the heart, hold the space for differences,* and *seek sincerity and brevity* in their own remarks.

We *listen and speak from the heart* when we evoke each other's stories with curiosity, wonder, and attention. A natural respect for all voices emerges in the process. For example, we don't fawn over one person's comments while curtly thanking or ignoring another. This can be a trap when there is a hierarchical culture underlying the gathering.

We *hold the space for differences* by inviting and honoring all points of view while seeking common ground. We let go of our assumptions—or at least recognize them for what they are—seeking to understand rather than persuade others of our own point of view. We all possess knowledge and make judgments that we believe are sensible, logical, honest, and true. However, beware of letting *what we know* get in the way of *what is so*.

Finally, we seek *sincerity and brevity* in our remarks. When we know that all voices will be heard, we can speak what has personal meaning to us and encourage all to do the same. We speak only from our own awareness and truth, often about what we are feeling/wondering at the moment. We make our words count because we respect the time for others to speak; yet we honor the need for our own full offering from the heart.

TALKING ABOUT THE WEATHER

Years ago, I learned a very important lesson about listening for the intent rather than the words. I'd just settled in Vermont with my family, moving down the road from a true Yankee farm family. One day, the father paid us a visit. After we shook hands, his eyes dropped to the gravel road, where he made patterns with his shoe. He then began talking about the weather. At first I thought, "Oh no, another shallow, self-conscious beginning to the conversation. Why doesn't he just get to the point and say why he stopped by?" It took me a few more visits before I learned what the gentle art of kicking the ground and talking about the weather was all about.

Humans are place-based creatures. The ground is our place, and the weather is the condition of the world around that place. This is very important to know about. Ever notice how many of your long-distance phone calls start with an exchange about the weather? What are you really saying to one another?

That old Vermonter taught me the etiquette of establishing a sense of place and an awareness of the condition of the world around both of us, prior to entering into whatever transaction we had. He taught me to have patience and listen for the deeper intent.

—By Craig Neal

PREPARING TO HEAR ALL THE VOICES

We prepare for this Aspect by asking ourselves how we will hear all the voices (what methods and practices we will use) while remembering who we are and for the sake of what we are gathering.

The focus of the Convener, at this point, is to be fully aware of who is in the room. We take into account the makeup of the constituents and the demographic characteristics, along with any psychological or emotional observations. Our goal is to "take the temperature" of the attendees in the gathering and to find common ground for questions.

The more that we are tuned to the people we are with, the more we are able to serve the present and future needs of the assembled.

A JOYFUL HEARING

Laurence headed the new-products division at a manufacturing company. He reported that his greatest revelation of the utility of the Art of Convening came with *Hearing All the Voices*.

When extra help was needed for a particular project, his company often hired temporary consultants or contractors. It was Laurence's experience, for some of these projects, that weeks of gnashing teeth, one-upping, resistance, and getting past prejudgments had to happen before useful collaboration could begin.

For a new-project launch meeting that would include everyone involved, Laurence decided to try the Art of Convening.

He prepared himself as best he could in the time he had. When it was time to think about *Hearing All the Voices*, he considered the different personalities that would be in the room that day. There would be the usual engineers, but also support people, designers, programmers, and project managers. A lot of information would be disseminated, with many people to hear from, just to "download" everyone's area of expertise and hear a short bio designed to let everyone know who would be doing what. He considered skipping *Hearing All the Voices* because of the time it would take and the discomfort it might cause some of the introverts in the room.

When the time came, however, he decided to include a "hearing." After welcoming everyone, *Setting Context*, and *Creating the Container* by laying out the protocols for the meeting, he said, "Well, we're all going to be working together for a while, and I don't know about you, but I'd like to know each of you a little better as we begin. So, right now, I'd like to go around the room and hear from each of you—one thing that brought joy to you today. It could be something that happens every day, or something unique. If nothing comes to you about today, just tell us something that has brought joy in the past. Take about 30 seconds or less. No more, since we have a lot to do today. I'll start."

Out of the corner of his eye, Laurence saw a couple of people look at each other with eyes rolling, but he didn't let that rattle him. He told of his drive to work that morning. He told them that as he crested a hill, the scene he saw of the sun coming up, creating a pink, otherworldly glow in the valley below, brought him a sense of joy and awe. That was all he said.

Each person spoke in turn, going around the room clockwise. One man told of his autistic son, who greeted him with a huge, heartfelt smile each morning. One woman told of her husband bringing her coffee to the bathroom because he knew she was in a hurry. Another told of the smell of lilacs in her driveway and another of lighthearted banter with the counter person at McDonald's that morning.

When everyone had spoken, Laurence looked around the room. There were lots of big smiles. People were looking at each other differently. They were "seeing" each other. There were no consultants, contractors, engineers, designers, or managers in the room at that moment—there were human beings.

As the meeting progressed, Laurence thought that some headway had already been made in the level of collaboration possible in this group. His courage in *Hearing All the Voices* had made a difference.[4]

GOOD QUESTIONS

When it is time for people to speak, the questions we invite them to address will form a basis for what we have come to do and create together. Framing good questions at the right time, in a container that has been safely formed, will greatly enhance the possibility for the group to reveal what is to be achieved together and the probability of its overall success.

The key is to find a question that is challenging enough to require thoughtful reflection, but that also evokes the commonality of the group. With a new group, simply asking each to speak his or her name and one or two words that describe his or her current condition may be sufficient to open the door to trust and what's next. Accessible everyday questions that put people at ease are crucial in the early stages of inviting everyone to speak. Parker Palmer, author of *A Hidden Wholeness: The Journey Toward an Undivided Life* (Jossey-Bass, 2009), reminds us of the "shy soul" that lives in each of us. Let's remember that for some people, public speaking can be intimidating.

We have observed that as people become more accustomed to speaking in a genuine and authentic way, the one-upmanship and competition to see who comes up with the wittiest or most interesting answer drops off, and a true appreciation and longing for simplicity and authenticity emerges.

STRINGING THE BEADS

One of the most elegant and efficient processes for *Hearing All the Voices* is an ancient yet thoroughly modern practice we've come to know as Stringing the Beads (see Exercise 1). The process is built on the metaphor that each person comes to any gathering as an individual, unique "bead." Each is as unique as a snowflake or a grain of sand. There are no two alike, never have been, nor will be. As defined, a bead has a hole in it through which thread is run to join it with other beads into a whole system. At the end of the process, we have strung a whole necklace, or string of beads, that did not exist before.

As each person speaks in turn, we lead ourselves to imagine a string slipping through the bead. When all of the voices have been heard, the string has gone through every bead, and the result is a beautiful "necklace" (or "bracelet," or other piece) that is a whole that did not exist at the beginning.

As Conveners, we create opportunities for wholeness to emerge from our individuality. This happens in our imagination, but it is a powerful instrument for creating a sense of wholeness in a group. Once we have strung the beads, we are energetically together and are prepared to engage in genuine, meaningful conversation. A more comprehensive step-by-step guide to Stringing the Beads can be found in the section "Arrows for Your Quiver," Arrow 1.

ON STRINGING THE BEADS

In our consulting firm, one of the ways we reinforce high standards and develop our ability to meet these standards is through monthly small-group meetings. As most of us are rarely in the office, these meetings are telephone conference calls. Membership and leadership of these small groups changes every three to six months. My opportunity to lead one of these groups came soon after I completed the Art of Convening series.

The calls bring senior leaders, consultants, and support staff together to discuss topics we are passionate about. Conversation is lively, but active participation by all is a challenge. Introducing the practice of Stringing the Beads at the beginning of the call enabled everyone to speak into the virtual circle and everyone's voice to be heard. I invited everyone in turn to say their name and where they were calling from, and then to share an experience about any opportunities they had to practice the previous month's topic.

A "stringing closure" provided an additional opportunity to hear all of our voices. Inviting each person to share a learning and/or an action to be taken as a result of the call ensured that people were listening, consciously knowing that they had a specific contribution to make before the end of the call.

Feedback has been very positive, and participants have shown keen interest in being a part of our group. My personal credibility as a Convener and facilitator continued to grow with this distinctive approach, although extending the concept to the other groups was more of a challenge. I can't say that this approach is used in all calls led by others, but calls where we String the Beads always results in a more lively and active conversation. Stringing the Beads provides a simple but effective way of giving everyone in our virtual circle a chance to speak, and creates the space for conversations that matter.

—By Paul G. Ward[5]

Where We Are on the Convening Wheel

1. *At the Heart of the Matter*—We have explored who we are and how we will be in relationship with others.
2. *Clarifying Intent*—We have identified an intention consistent with *At the Heart of the Matter* that has substance and is acted upon.
3. *The Invitation*—We have extended a sincere invitation with genuine hospitality, generosity, and conviction.
4. *Setting Context*—We have clearly communicated the form, function, and purpose of our gathering.
5. *Creating the Container*—We have prepared a physical space with beauty and life, and we have agreed on terms of engagement or protocols that bring safety for our time together.
6. *Hearing All the Voices*—We have spoken and heard every other person speak in our gathering, creating an authentic whole.

We have now heard all the voices in our gathering. Next we begin one of the most exciting Aspects of our convening: *Essential Conversation*. We have set the table and said grace (so to speak). Now it is time to feast.

Things to Remember

Challenge: *Impatience/judgment*

Principle: *Each voice is needed to reveal the best outcome of our engagement.*

Essential Questions:

- Who are we, and what have we come to say and do together?

- How will we hear all the voices at this gathering?
- What methods and practices will allow for the full expression of all participants?

Aspect-Strengthening Exercises

Checklist for the Gathering at Hand

- Do I know what method I will use when *Hearing All the Voices?*
- What question will I ask that will have everyday meaning to all participants?
- Remind yourself and all who are gathered:
    1. I seek to be interested rather than interesting.
    2. I seek to understand and be of service.
    3. I seek to speak from the heart, succinctly and with clarity.

EXERCISE 1: STRINGING THE BEADS—SHORT FORM[6]

At your next gathering or meeting, tell people you'd like to start the meeting by hearing from each of them, because each person counts and our voices are a way for us to bring ourselves into the meeting. You may refer to it as being "present and accounted for." If it is appropriate for the group, use the terminology of Stringing the Beads. The first time may bring nervous laughter and a few remarks. Once you've moved beyond this point, it's usually clear sailing.

Step 1. Ask each to say, in turn, as you go around the circle, his or her name and a few words in reply to either "What's been going on for you today?" or "What's been a positive moment you can remember today?" Something easy and fun is best to get started. Be sure to say how much time each has to speak. This can be as long or as short as you have time for. Thirty to 60 seconds is usually sufficient.

Step 2. When they are finished speaking, ask them to let the group know by saying "I have spoken" or "I am finished," so that the group knows they are finished and not just pausing.

Once everyone has spoken, thank them and remark how much you learned. You might ask for brief thoughts or feedback. Notice the difference in the energy of the meeting. Now it's time to begin the meeting.

Closing the meeting: Leave time at the end to close the session with a quick second round of "stringing." We all like to know when a meeting formally begins and ends. People appreciate the practice and soon ask for the "stringing" closure if we forget. Most of us love to be heard. For the closing, ask for a simple few words in reply to "What will you take from this meeting that is significant or important" or "What is one insight or tool you'll be able to use from this meeting?" Again, remind people how much time each has to speak. This can be as long or as short as you have time for.

There are many ways in which to achieve the desired result. If the language of Stringing the Beads seems awkward or "out there" to the group, then don't use it right away or at all. The important aspect of the practice is to give voice to each member of the meeting or gathering at the beginning and the end. These simple words at the opening and closing may in fact be the most important words uttered at the meeting. Genuine expressions of interest and gratitude go a long way toward opening the door to our creativity and loyalty to each other.

EXERCISE 2: DEEP LISTENING AND RESPONSE

Remember to do the following:

- Seek to understand and be of service
- Be interested rather than interesting
- Honor the mundane in creating common ground

Next time you run into a neighbor, friend, or family member, start the conversation with a comment about the weather or your home or family. Be conscious of your opening, and listen to the response. Then ask a question about that person's current condition. How is that person doing, really? Then listen and respond, if appropriate, in kind. Notice how the rest of the exchange moves along. The same can be done with business associates.

If we honor the miracle of everyday life by being interested rather than needing to be interesting, even the most mundane conversation can turn into a transformative experience for all. People love to be heard. It's all in the simple things.

Journaling Questions

- How are you creating opportunities for authentic engagement, in which all the voices are heard, in your life and work?
- What have you noticed about the quality and outcomes of your engagements when the essence of the interchange has depth and meaning as opposed to when it does not?
- Think of a time when you have engaged in Stringing the Beads outside of a convened environment. What happened?

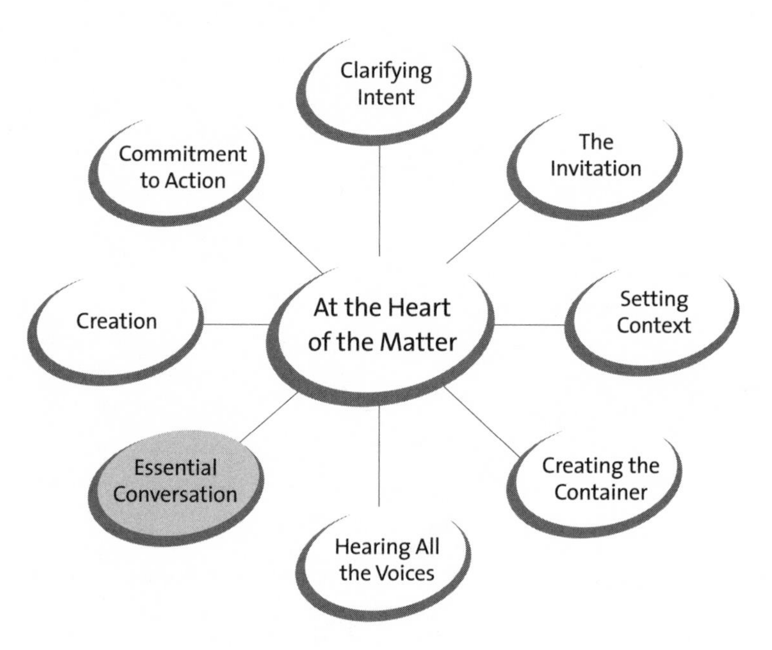
Clarifying Intent
The Invitation
Setting Context
Creating the Container
Hearing All the Voices
Essential Conversation
Creation
Commitment to Action
At the Heart of the Matter

7. ESSENTIAL CONVERSATION

Meaningful exchange in an atmosphere of trust

HAVING CONVERSATIONS OF CONSEQUENCE

Essential Conversation is, in many ways, the meat of authentic engagement. In order to get there, we follow the Aspects of the Convening Wheel that come before so that we may gracefully enter *Essential Conversation* with planning and respect. The presence of trust and safety plays an important role in the quality of the conversation and the ability to maintain authenticity.

When we're authentic and engaged, we're more able and willing to work together to imagine, and be responsible for, the best possible future. When creativity and wisdom become activated, whatever outcomes the group is working toward can be enhanced or accelerated.

Once the container has been successfully created and we've begun with hearing the voices of the assembled, there is an opening for a graceful transition to the very practical Aspect of *Essential Conversation*.

Various potent dialogic and conversational methods (World Café, Bohmian Dialogue, Appreciative Inquiry, and Circle Process, to name a few) can be good tools for establishing *Essential Conversation*. Two methods we use are the following: asking for reflections "popcorn style" (that is, each person in the gathering speaks whenever he or she is moved to speak, in what sometimes seems like a verbal "popping") and small-group breakouts. In both settings, conversation is initiated with an invitation to speak or a directed question to speak to. We remind participants of the protocols of engagement, utilizing the Principles of Conversation, such as deep listening, slowing down the conversation, and allowing the space for difference (see "Arrows for Your Quiver"). The crucial step now is to call upon the participants to share their wholehearted wisdom with each other.

A critical challenge at this juncture is self-consciousness. It may show up as internal mind chatter exhibiting itself as nervous domination over the conversation, or as not speaking at all. Ultimately, this behavior prevents us from being vulnerable and genuine in our exchanges. As Conveners, we are vigilant for the signs of self-consciousness in ourselves and the participants. Establishing and reestablishing trust is the key to overcoming this challenge so that the gifts of authentic engagement and our wholehearted wisdom can emerge.

Once in *Essential Conversation*, the Convener is called on to use whatever skills we have acquired personally and professionally (leadership, facilitation, coaching, and training) to detect and work with the reluctance and/or anxiety that comes with self-consciousness. The goal is to keep all participants involved.

We're now three-quarters of the way around the Convening Wheel, having moved from the more preparatory Aspects of the engagement to the most socially engaged point of the meeting. The foundation for trust and respect has been laid, opening the possibility of experiencing our interdependence and the best common future we can imagine together. Because we have taken the time to prepare the seedbed of our engagement, an environment has been created where there is excellent potential for everyone to be energetically connected as part of a whole living system.

CHALLENGE

Self-consciousness

The principal challenge in this Aspect of our gathering is self-consciousness (awkwardness or embarrassment in the presence of others; being ill at ease). It might look like eyes averted or heads down, or show up as either not speaking or speaking without listening. However it is exhibited, in us or others, facing up to the nature of self-consciousness is critical in order to maintain authentic engagement that provides the meaningful exchange that is *Essential Conversation.*

Slowing things down and getting back to familiar territory, as in *Hearing All the Voices,* is one way to address self-consciousness in a group. Another is to honestly admit our own self-consciousness and model our own courageous willingness to move beyond it. Whatever way we choose to address this challenge, we do our best to ease fears and model respectful authenticity.

EXTROVERT/INTROVERT DILEMMA

Pam convened a regular meeting of leaders in a large health-care organization. She reported that her convening muscles were most exercised during the *Essential Conversation* part of the meeting.

Once she had brought the group through *Hearing All the Voices* and opened the group to discussion of the topic at hand, there was a tendency for the two or three extroverts in the group to do all the talking. The three or four introverts, perhaps self-conscious or uncomfortable with interrupting, seemed content to sit and listen.

When she noticed this happening, she would pause the group. "Let's stop for a minute. We can continue to discuss this issue, but right now I'd like to go around and hear an opinion from everyone. Then we can open it up again."

Sometimes one of the extroverts would again begin to dominate the meeting, but Pam had learned to be very clear about the terms of engagement, while honoring each participant. "We want to hear your thoughts, but right now the process is to hear from everyone. Don't worry, you will have a chance to say what you need to say."

Pam held the people in a container of safety and trust, and allowed the full expression of wisdom to emerge from the group.[1]

PRINCIPLE

Meaningful exchange creates a connected and interdependent whole.

When our conversation lacks meaning, as when we exchange clichés or just "download" our thoughts onto others without listening or understanding, we remain disconnected from those around us even in the midst of what we might consider a fun and lively conversation. Introducing thoughtfulness and meaning into what we say and how we hear others brings us to realize our connection.

When we sense our interdependency, we see that our future is tied together. Authentic engagement is then more likely to continue. Participating in meaningful exchange is a powerful way to make this interdependency salient to all.

ESSENTIAL QUESTIONS

Has the ground been adequately laid for essential conversation to occur?

What am I now aware of or open to (that perhaps I was not before)?

What wisdom is already present?

These are the questions we ask ourselves as we move from *Hearing All the Voices* to *Essential Conversation*. The first question requires us to assess whether the ground is adequately laid for the *Essential Conversation* to begin (for example, people are not talking, or there are latecomers who missed the first part); then we may choose to go back to *Hearing All the Voices* for another round, or restate context, agreements, or intentions.

We also ask ourselves what we are now aware of that we were not before. It might be something that a participant said during *Hearing All the Voices*, or it might be a shift in the energy of the group itself that we detect. The time may also be right for us to notice how our own perceptions and positions create receptivity to the group.

We want to approach *Essential Conversation* in a way that flows naturally for the participants, and the answers to these questions will allow us to determine what is best, trusting that everything we need to know is already present in the room.

MAKING IT REAL

There are many ways to bring our group into *Essential Conversation*. If we've done our preparation thoroughly, the purpose for our gathering is clear to everyone. The group has begun to connect more seriously through *Hearing All the Voices* and is now mentally, emotionally, and energetically ready to engage at a more essential level. One way to enter *Essential Conversation* is to open the floor for reflections or comments. Conversation can be initiated with an invitation to speak freely or a directed question to speak to. The Convener must decide how best to frame this interaction. Still another way to enter into *Essential Conversation* is to ask particular people to comment or ask to hear from each participant in turn.

"LET THE WILD RUMPUS BEGIN"

A powerful way to get to *Essential Conversation*, especially with larger gatherings, is to split the group into smaller groups of three to five people. Using the Principles of Conversation (see "Arrows for Your Quiver") as a group-process guide, these small groups can effectively, with the aid of good themes or questions, bring the participants to recognize each other as fellow travelers. These small, "knee to knee" groups also encourage deep listening and sharing. At the Thought Leader Gatherings and in other settings, we call these Wisdom Circles. The process is created to evoke the wisdom of the participants.

Coming back from a round or two of these small-group sessions, the Convener may ask for reflections or reports back from each individual, certain individuals, or anyone who is ready to speak.

OUR LEADERSHIP IS NEEDED

Although this Aspect of the Convening Wheel is the place where participants gain independent energy to continue, the Convener's job is not over. This is where our skills as leaders, facilitators, coaches, or trainers come in to help us manage this sometimes-messy phase of our engagement. Our objective is to remain alert for self-consciousness and to get to the place where people are willing and ready to work together authentically.

CREATING MEANING AT WORK

As a group of cautious but willing learners, we stumbled through a new way of being together at work. The process provided an increasing recognition that convening and having a language and a process to generate solutions to our issues brought empowerment and built trust. We did not set out to "create" anything in particular, but one of the most powerful impacts was learning that having a place where you can have meaningful conversations creates power.

Most compelling was where we arrived after six months. We had, through this process, become a "community." The principles and practices set us up to demonstrate care, create true understanding, and share thoughts and ideas in a productive manner. We made commitments to bring forward what we valued and what we saw as needed in our organization. We shared what we were learning with our peers and our clients, we told stories of our success, and we recommitted to our next series of applications and actions.

In terms of building capability, the skills, tools, and application of the Art of Convening principles and practices are still being used. The business benefits are both tangible and intangible as the HR organization continues to meet with greater efficiency and effectiveness. I find it interesting that in business, we typically shy away from getting to the heart of the matter, yet what we learned through this experience was that being with the heart of the matter is where true performance contributions manifest and become significant business impacts.

—By Anne Griswold[2]

When we notice that the participants are tending toward self-consciousness, signaled by individual or collective agitation, reluctance to engage, or disharmony, we may choose to bring the group back together by convening another Transition Exercise (see chapter 4), Stringing the Beads again, or restating the terms of engagement. The Convener, as leader, evaluates all the elements of the gathering—the unique characteristics of the participants, the design and venue—and makes a clear-headed assessment of our own personal capacities, skills, and expertise. As with driving a car, the more we practice convening, the more natural and instinctive these decisions become.

The continuation of trust through integrity is the key for the success of this Aspect. What is wanted from people here is their wholehearted engagement and wisdom. This can happen very easily and naturally; however, the journey can also be emotional and messy. Remember, the Convener does not fix situations or people to make either better. The Convener's role is to steward the space for participants to offer their gifts.

TRUST

Trust is born in an environment that allows for personal safety and truth telling. When we know what the agreed-upon game is and trust that what we are hearing from people is true, the possibility for authentic or *Essential Conversation* is present. When the dialogue is trusted to be authentic, or at least the cards are on the table, the mood in the gathering transforms from one of perhaps confusion, mistrust, or even hostility to collegiality. It is then possible for the participants to have a sense that they belong to the same community.

Achieving trust is no small thing. We live in a world where the rationale for our distrust is constantly reinforced. It's so ingrained in our psyches that we don't normally question the validity of our distrust.

There is a cost to this distrust and caution in our everyday relationships, and therefore our engagements. If we expend energy trying to second-guess the virtue and validity of everything we hear and experience from others, we have less energy to be truly engaged and creative. That's why the preparatory work, in the sequencing of the Wheel, is so important. A potent antidote to fear and distrust is having an experience that proves otherwise. What we have created is a space for give and take. Authentic engagement thrives in this kind of environment.

Imagine now that we've successfully created a safe and trusting container in which to have our meeting. The assembled have all introduced themselves, and spoken to their goals and aspirations for the gathering. The last person has spoken, and now the room is silent. Imagine what the people in the group may be thinking and feeling. This is the moment when a transformative shift is most potent.

In more cases than not, an *Arc of Recognition* takes place (see the next section). It may have already occurred during the time of *Hearing All the Voices*, and it allows for *Essential Conversation* to take place.

ARC OF RECOGNITION

When we are invited to speak our name and what is true for us, and we hear others do the same, an energetic shift predictably occurs that is at once quite ordinary and simultaneously astoundingly transformative for the group. We wrote in the preceding chapter about the power of being heard. However, the combination of speaking and listening deeply in a safe container produces a remarkable shift within a group that may be imperceptible to almost everyone but the Convener. Simply put, we experience being heard and "seen" as *who we truly are* while simultaneously seeing and hearing others for *who they are*. This produces the effect of recognizing one another in an essential way. In the movie *Avatar*, the central social theme revolved around the indigenous Na'vi "seeing" one another. This sweet spot in any gathering is a moment that the Convener watches for with great anticipation. It's the appearance of this *Arc of Recognition* that can enable us to successfully enter *Essential Conversation*.

More specifically, something is happening in the group dynamics. Like much in life, it's the simple things that often have the greatest impact. When we are asked to speak from a place of meaning and allowed the space to do so, we become vulnerable and open to each other as witnesses to who we really are. This is true even if we are just saying our name, where we live, and a word or two about our present condition. Hearing others speak this way may have the effect of creating a shared experience—an *arc* across the room (or space)—that allows us to truly recognize our common humanity. With practice and deepening of our own awareness and skills, we facilitate this authentic engagement more and more. It may happen in the first Stringing of the Beads, or when we open to *Essential Conversation*, or perhaps further along in the engagement, if there is a second Stringing or beyond. We then have the potential to experience interdependence and a common future. A very natural trust emanates from this awareness, allowing authentic engagement, leading to the potential for our collective wisdom.

STILL THE VOICE INSIDE

As I have brought Art of Convening principles to my program planning and evaluation work, it has been exciting to see movement from stale meetings to participatory processes where the energy level and sense of possibility is palpable. I once had the difficult job of helping an organization examine their mission and values, which ultimately ended a youth mentoring component of their program that was not working well. Using principles from the AoC, such as knowing myself as a Convener and approaching each session by preparing a safe container for each participant, I helped the group decide for themselves how their organization should evolve.

I developed a step-by-step process over a period of several weeks that allowed the mentoring program to end gracefully. The process culminated in a circle where each Native American youth shared about their time with their mentor. These youth, who for the most part had not been very communicative to their mentors about their feelings, did an amazing job of eloquently expressing their reflections in this circle, including unsolicited but very insightful comments about their own participation. This experience included the difficult practice for me to "still the voice inside" that wants to move to a solution too quickly and left me with a sense of awe about the power of respectful convening.

—By Lauren Patterson[3]

The art, for the Convener, is in the recognition of the subtle shift of energy and in knowing what to do or not do in the moment. Our inner work, drawn from the initial aspects of the Wheel, comes in handy here. Since we can't count on anyone else to have done the preparation or to be on the lookout for these vital signs, this is the moment when our skills of patience and discernment pay off. As the Conveners, we are continually sensing the mood of the group. We assess the energy and the ability of the assembled to be connected—both personally and to their common future. This is usually the time to slow down the conversation and find common ground. At this stage, the participants may engage with one another, for the first time, in a meaningful way and begin to function as a unified "living system."

The phenomenon of the *Arc of Recognition* has been experienced many times in Thought Leader Gatherings (TLGs). Embedded in the design of each of the half-day sessions is the seed of *Essential Conversation,* which rarely fails to come to full blossom. Take note of the progression of the Aspects as you read about the TLG format.

THOUGHT LEADER GATHERINGS

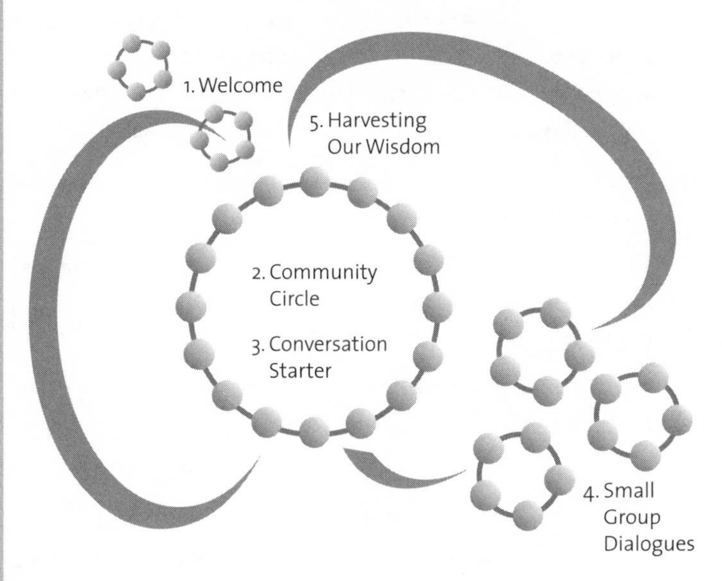

Heartland has convened Thought Leader Gatherings every month since their founding in 1998. These events alternate between the San Francisco Bay Area of California and the Twin Cities area of Minnesota.

How the Gatherings Work

Each phase of the four-hour Thought Leader Gathering (TLG) is designed to bring the group to an experience of the Arc of Recognition, which then stimulates and reveals the collective wisdom of the group in an effective and efficient, yet unhurried, time frame. We draw on ancient as well as modern group process models, borrowing from the great cultural and organizational traditions.

The TLGs are held in beautiful venues that offer access to natural lighting and wholesome food. The format is designed to guide the 50–100 participants successfully through an interactive learning experience, from the conversation starter's opening remarks to the closing harvesting session. The hub of each gathering is the Community Circle, where the conversations begin and end.

The Elements of Design

The day begins with breakfast at round tables of six to eight. In an adjacent space is a large Community Circle with a chair for each participant, which will, throughout the session, be reconfigured into small-group Wisdom Circles (see "Arrows for Your Quiver"). The day proceeds as follows:

- Everyone is welcomed by a greeter at registration.
- The session starts with a welcome, followed by *Setting Context* for the gathering, including a brief genesis story of how the TLG began, and the agenda/overview of the day.
- We communicate the agreements, including an agreement to utilize the Principles of Conversation.
- A brief transition exercise follows, then an invitation to join the Community Circle.
- Once in the circle, we String the Beads for *Hearing All the Voices*.
- We introduce the conversation starter (presenter), and he or she speaks.
- Break.
- Two rounds of small-group Wisdom Circles follow the break, shuffling participants and addressing different questions.
- We return to the Community Circle to Harvest the Wisdom.

This core design has been convened in this essential form each month for 12 consecutive years in Minnesota and California, with consistent results that many experience as transformational.

The journey around the Convening Wheel is made prior to, in the planning of, and during each TLG. The process is initiated by clarifying our purpose and intention into a compelling integral invitation. The venue has been prepared to maximize safety, beauty, and interaction. The flow of activity from the welcome;

through *Setting Context*, agreements, and protocols; to *Hearing All the Voices* is seamless.

The goal, once again, is to create the container in which each can experience the Arc of Recognition. It may come early in the session, during Stringing the Beads, or later, during the small-group Wisdom Circles, or back in the large circle as we Harvest the Wisdom.

Bringing a room full of people together, from longtime members to first-timers, month after month, to achieve a high level of *Essential Conversation* that matters demands an ability to create and execute a design of convening principles and practices that are consistently effective.

We have seen over and over again that when the conditions are set for meaningful engagement, the potential for the individual to viscerally experience a connection to and interdependence with others increases many-fold.

WHERE WE ARE ON THE CONVENING WHEEL

1. *At the Heart of the Matter*—We have explored who we are and how we will be in relationship with others.
2. *Clarifying Intent*—We have identified an intention consistent with *At the Heart of the Matter* that has substance and is acted upon.
3. *The Invitation*—We have extended a sincere invitation with genuine hospitality, generosity, and conviction.
4. *Setting Context*—We have clearly communicated the form, function, and purpose of our gathering.
5. *Creating the Container*—We have prepared a physical space with beauty and life, and we have agreed on terms of engagement or protocols that bring safety for our time together.
6. *Hearing All the Voices*—We have spoken and heard every other person speak in our gathering, creating an authentic whole.
7. *Essential Conversation*—We have entered into a meaningful exchange in an atmosphere of trust.

Essential Conversation is an exciting phase of our engagement that has power and consequence. As this conversation develops, a key outcome will be the subject of the next chapter—*Creation*.

Things to Remember

Challenge: *Self-consciousness. Are we willing to be seen and listen deeply enough to see others?*

Principle: *Meaningful exchange creates a connected and interdependent whole.*

Essential Questions:

- Has the ground been adequately laid for essential conversation to occur?
- What am I now aware of or open to (that perhaps I was not before)?
- What wisdom is already present?

Aspect-Strengthening Exercises

Checklist for the Gathering at Hand

- Do a mood check of the group. Have you heard all the voices?
- This is usually a good time to slow down the conversation to find the common ground.
- Are there energy leaks in the group? Check for signs of self-conscious behavior.
- Are you able to sense the presence of the Arc of Recognition?
- Assess the energy and ability of the group to be connected—personally and to their common future.
- Are you ready to move on to *Creation*?

EXERCISE 1: CONVERSATION REDIRECT AND REFLECTION

The next time you find yourself in a conversation with another person and you wish to shift the exchange from superficial to one of more depth, try the following:

1. Simply ask your partner if it's OK to hit the pause button for a moment or two of silence to reflect on why you decided to meet. This reflective "time-in" encourages the possibility of meaningful and transformative conversation.

2. Now briefly share with your partner what came up for you; then ask your partner to do the same.

Reflection is a core leadership competency. Designing opportunities for taking a time-in to reflect has the effect of slowing down the interaction to the speed of life, therefore allowing for a deeper consideration of the purpose of your interaction with that person. With reflection comes listening, which births understanding. Wisdom is the outcome.

EXERCISE 2: PRACTICING MEANINGFUL EXCHANGE

1. Find a private and comfortable place to sit close to and directly across from one other person.
2. Decide who will speak first to a predetermined question of mutual interest. Speak of things in your everyday life that have real meaning for you; resist exchanging cliché for cliché.
3. Now look directly into each other's eyes, and take turns speaking and listening without interruption or distraction.
4. The speaker speaks for a few minutes while the listener simply listens, offering no verbal or physical feedback. When the first speaker is finished, simply thank one another and switch roles.
5. You may alternate speaking and listening for as long as you wish.
6. Remember, it is important to avoid advice giving or feedback. You may wish to go offline if things come up that you feel you need to further work through together.

Journaling Questions

- Recall a time when you engaged in a meaningful conversation in an atmosphere of trust. How was this different from other conversations?
- When in your life have you experienced the Arc of Recognition in relationship to your engagements—of being seen by others in your essence while simultaneously knowing that others are having the same experience?

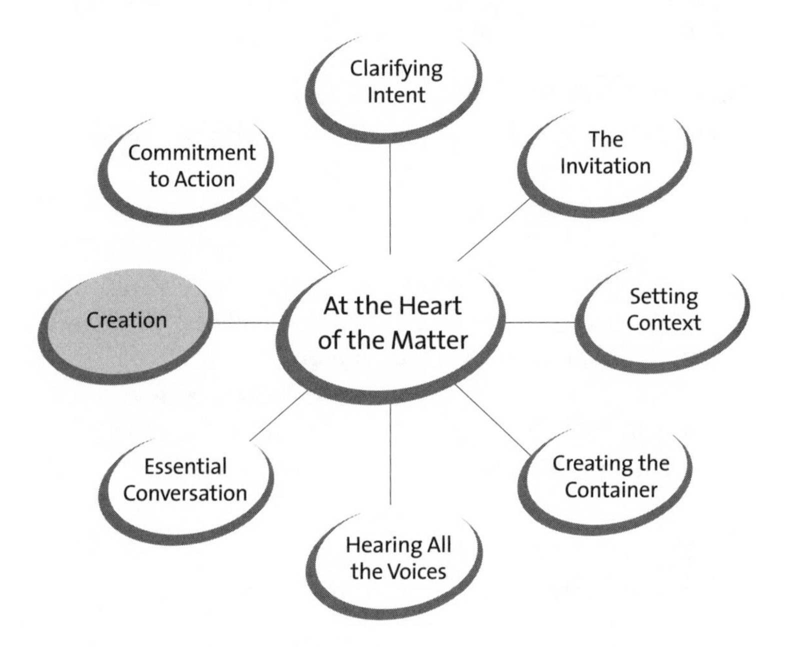
Clarifying Intent
The Invitation
Setting Context
Creating the Container
Hearing All the Voices
Essential Conversation
Creation
Commitment to Action
At the Heart of the Matter

8. CREATION

Something new that emerges from engagements of shared purpose and trust

WHAT IS CREATION?

Creation, in the context of convening, is something new that emerges in our gathering as a result of authentic engagement during *Essential Conversation*. We don't know what the creation will be, and it is out of our direct control. We can, however, plan, nurture, and set the conditions in which it emerges, just as a gardener fosters the conditions for a plant to emerge from the ground.

> WHEN WE *are listened to, it creates us, makes us unfold and expand.*
>
> —*Brenda Ueland*[1]

Depending on the purpose of our gathering, the creation could be a new product idea, a new marketing concept, or a way for the family to be together more meaningfully. It could also be a thought, a revelation about our relationship with others, or a modification of something old (which makes it new!). Whatever the form of the creation, it is the role of the Convener to attentively keep the participants authentically engaged so that they are able to generate the new. The Convener intervenes only under certain circumstances—if the group seems to be getting disengaged, the container needs to be strengthened, or the new emerging themes need emphasis or illumination.

Conveners all have unique personal tools, abilities, and training. When we enter the Aspect of *Creation*, we use these personal assets to bring the group members into awareness of their commonality and their collective, creative imagination.

AUTHENTIC ENGAGEMENT IS KEY

When we authentically engage, we are not recycling old dialogue or behavior; we're tapping what is true for us now, at this moment. Our authenticity allows us to bring a presence to the engagement that is unique to this moment in time. This unique presence means that what is occurring in our gathering has never happened before. If we have followed the Aspects of the Convening Wheel and have entered *Essential Conversation*, every participant in our gathering is bringing this unique presence. Therefore, something new must emerge.

CHALLENGE

Disengagement

For the Aspect of *Creation* to emerge within the gathering, the Convener and all participants continue to authentically engage, remaining present and open to others' ideas, in order to move forward energetically. Disengagement may threaten our gathering in the form of distraction, dissent, inertia, resistance, or criticism.

The Convener recognizes that something special is happening and, while allowing the process to continue, remains vigilant to the surroundings and the mood of the group. At this point, the group may veer off in a distracting direction, which would open the door for it to become energetically or psychically disengaged. The Convener is watchful at this juncture to protect the safety of the group so that the participants remain willing to move forward in trust.

This is a time when a participant may challenge the direction of the group or the authority of the Convener. The Convener may bring the conversation back to the center, or remind the participants of the *context, protocols,* and *agreements,* while honoring dissent within a container of freedom. The important role for the Convener at this time is to protect the integrity of the container, reinforce the context, and notice the creation that is emerging.

PRINCIPLE

The emergence of something new that did not exist before is the root of innovation and meaningful contribution.

We elicit the emergence of something new because that is why we have engaged with others in the first place. We may have gathered because we are interested in deeper connection, learning, finding better ways to collaborate, solving problems together, or strengthening our relationships. As human beings, we also long to share our unique gifts. Implicit in our meeting is the expectation that something will happen that transforms us, that we will not be the same coming out as we were going in.

When something new emerges from our gathering, whether it is new thinking or a full-blown treatise, the possibility of our making a meaningful contribution to our shared future is greatly enhanced.

Out there in the air,
there is a field where fresh ideas come and go.
Joining, we start to move with new frequency
in relationship with ourselves,
with others, and even the field itself.

Moving more freely, we see new things;
and the old, familiar views, a-new.
This opening, this broad space,
is the place of letting go, of running,
where so much is born.

We see a beautiful, broad field in red-orange-yellow.

We've entered this broad space, by design.
Leaving all we know behind hoping to find
what we are looking for:
Big thinking, brainstorming, ideation.
Rhythm. Relationship.

It is in this open,
seemingly boundless place,
that things often get too open.
Too loud, too fast, too loose.
A little . . . wild.

ESSENTIAL QUESTIONS

What are we to create together?

How will I recognize and harvest the wisdom being created?

What is the new that we can bring back to our relationships and communities, personal and organizational?

Convention and rules fall away.
The wilding ideas run and spin.
We dance, alone, together.
Dizzy and tripping, we go
from "free" to sometimes "amuck."
What? "Others don't see things as we do?"

We shout, we struggle for our footing, for the other.

The sun goes behind the clouds
and all the colors turn to brown,
then gray . . . then black.

We've gone a-field on purpose.
In this darkness, we know.
Still we know.
That this is the place.
This place here—

Way out here—
where grace and alchemy roam
amid the shadows;
where creativity
and meaningful work
are forged of togetherness.

—Elizabeth Becker[3]

As Conveners, we ask ourselves these questions as we enter into this Aspect and take note of what we recognize as new. Our own creativity, practiced and honed, will allow us to recognize the emerging new more reliably.

It is helpful for us to recognize and capture the new entity that emerges from our gathering; however, sometimes the emerging new is invisible to us. It could be a shift in thinking or an old idea revisited. Quite often, the obvious is staring us in the face, and all we need to do is recognize it. There are many ways to harvest the wisdom being created, if that is what's called for, and different methods at our disposal, depending on our area of expertise, training, or preference. We ask ourselves what method will be best for this gathering.

MAKING IT REAL

We communicated the purpose for our meeting at the beginning and so have primed the participants to be in the best state of mind for that purpose. But we still don't know what form our creation together will take. The Convener listens to the participants and is alert for repeating themes and commonality in their collective, creative imagination.

WHEN THE BOTTOM DROPS OUT

It was toward the end of a two-day training session retreat when the bottom seemed to drop out of the container of safety of the group. They were a hierarchically oriented work group who had come to the session with deep-seated issues around trust and cynicism.

Over time, we were able to tap into our individual and collective stories and open the door to the possibility of a shared future that all could get behind.

We worked hard, made and struck agreements, articulated the context of our intent, and heard all the voices time and again; the shell of fear and sarcasm began to crack open. We found our common values and visions emerging quite gracefully. A palpable sense of shared wisdom and trust emerged in the room.

Then, suddenly, following a particularly vulnerable sharing by one of the members, a cloud of dread came over the group. This person fled the room crying while others turned to me, in panic, for answers. I could feel the collective good will being mightily tested.

Some asked me why this had happened, what was said, and who was to blame. Others visibly tightened and withdrew. I knew this was a reality test for the group. Could they believe what they had created or not? Could they endure the exposure to authentic conversation and courage demanded of the group to achieve the level of commitment they were on the verge of making together?

Did they, as a group, have the courage to sit in the discomfort and hold one another during this meltdown?

Did I, as Convener, trust in my own internal preparation enough to hold my own doubts and fears as well as those of the group?

As the Convener, I had to decide what to do. My instincts told me to move forward with this group as planned and to trust the bond we were forming to get us through this.

After a short break, I reconvened the group, sat in silence, and then asked the person who had left the room if she wished to share what was going on with her. Her response was refreshingly honest and straightforward; she said that what she had experienced was a breakthrough in confronting her fear about being seen for who she really was, and that for a moment she had been afraid that she would be judged as weak and ineffective. The result was overpowering. Her admission and candor spoke volumes to the rest of the group. The level of empathy and identification with her fear was universal.

The heavy cloud of apprehension lifted from the room immediately.

Now we were ready to lean into one another as a tested and tempered interdependent whole. The work we did for the remainder of the retreat and our time together was forever changed in those few minutes. Powerful!

—By Craig Neal

Conscious nurturing is the main theme for the *Creation* Aspect. When we prepare the soil for planting, place our seeds, water, and weed, something eventually grows. In a sense, we have facilitated the growth of something new. Of course, plants grow all the time without anyone doing anything. In fact, it's almost impossible to prevent some plants from growing—yet our nurturing influences what grows where, and how vigorously. We come to this Aspect because we want to encourage growth where there is none, we want to encourage a different kind of growth, or we want to culture and refine the growth we have.

In our gathering so far, we've engaged in setting the stage for this growth that emerges spontaneously within a nurturing, well-formed container that has shaped it.

This is a time for subtlety and nuanced activity from the Convener. The hand of intervention is used consciously and wisely. Witnessing creation of the essential kind, when something new is born from the collective expression of those gathered, is like witnessing the initial sprout of a plant emerging from the earth. This is a time when we pay close attention to the vital signs of the people; whether the container is holding is crucial. The group may test the strength of one another and of the container itself.

When our gathering hovers here, between the Aspects of *Essential Conversation* and *Commitment to Action*, the experience may be subtle or wrenching. If we've done our work well, the group will almost take care of itself, no matter how explosive and passionate the creative process may be.

CAPTURING THE CREATIVE IMPULSE

Recognizing and capturing this creation can be obvious or elusive. Our personal and professional field of practice in which we work with the creative process can be very helpful in honing our ability to detect the emerging new. Relying on our common sense and being awake to the subtle or obvious shifts of group energy can help us to recognize the emerging new in our gathering.

Here are some things to look for now:

- Are the vast majority of the people engaged? If not, who is not and why not? A gentle hand or intervention may be appropriate to bring outliers in or utilize their contribution.
- Do you sense agreement, conflict, or indecision, or are people still in process? Be aware of these three forms of group dynamics. Are you ready to move on, step back, or wait a while longer?
- What is waiting to be born that may be on the tips of people's tongues but as yet unspoken?

Capturing the new, or bringing the group to awareness of it in a useful way, is also a function that the Convener serves. We use whatever tools we have at our disposal to draw, record, write, or emphasize the emergent new. We use our background in coaching, facilitation, or teaching to ask questions of the participants, or to illuminate the new for them—if they have not already recognized the new on their own.

Now is the time to put on your facilitator's hat! There are many ways and methodologies you can use to reveal the gifts that are individually and collectively waiting to be offered. As we suggested in chapter 7, on *Essential Conversation,* we use the technique, process, or methodology that suits our culture, the objectives of the meeting, and our experience level. *The Change Handbook: Group Methods for Shaping the Future,* by Tom Devane and Peggy Holman (Berrett-Koehler Publishers, 1999), offers an especially comprehensive overview of group process methodologies.

HOLDING ON AND LETTING GO

The creative process is messy at times, explosive at others, and occasionally we may find it easy paddling.

The Art *in* Convening, an instinctive knowing that develops with practice, is very helpful during this Aspect of the Wheel. It's where expectations are the greatest and the demand for presence is most profound. Consider the tree in the midst of the hurricane, able to stay firmly rooted yet bending and swaying to the overpowering wind, allowing the force of change to wash over it.

The Convener fiercely holds the integrity of the container, honoring the individuals in relationship with one another, in community, so that the new that emerges is consistent with the purpose, heart, and values of this community.

Where We Are on the Convening Wheel

1. *At the Heart of the Matter*—We have explored who we are and how we will be in relationship with others.
2. *Clarifying Intent*—We have identified an intention consistent with *At the Heart of the Matter* that has substance and is acted upon.
3. *The Invitation*—We have extended a sincere invitation with genuine hospitality, generosity, and conviction.
4. *Setting Context*—We have clearly communicated the form, function, and purpose of our gathering.
5. *Creating the Container*—We have prepared a physical space with beauty and life, and we have agreed on terms of engagement or protocols that bring safety for our time together.
6. *Hearing All the Voices*—We have spoken and heard every other person speak in our gathering, creating an authentic whole.
7. *Essential Conversation*—We have entered into a meaningful exchange in an atmosphere of trust.
8. *Creation*—We have observed and nurtured the emergence of something new in our gathering.

When we are in the *Creation* Aspect of the Convening Wheel, we know that we've done our preparation well. Our gathering is coming to an end, and we move to "capture" this energy and wisdom generated by participants as we enter the next Aspect, *Commitment to Action*.

Things to Remember

Challenge: *Disengagement.* Is everyone engaged?

Principle: *The emergence of something that did not exist before is the root of innovation and meaningful contribution.*

Essential Questions:

- What are we to create together?
- How will I recognize and harvest the wisdom being created?
- What is the new that we can bring back to our relationships and communities, personal and business?

Aspect-Strengthening Exercises

Checklist for the Gathering at Hand

- Am I prepared to recognize the new when it emerges in this gathering?
- Am I prepared to harvest the new when and if it emerges?
- What method will be used to "hold the people"—to keep everyone engaged as creation happens?

EXERCISE 1: CHILD'S PLAY OR BEGINNER'S MIND

Overview

Ever notice how uninhibited young children under the age of six are? How they seem to assume connection to one another and the world around them as given? There is something to relearn here. We call it innocence or beginner's mind, referring to having an attitude of openness, eagerness, and lack of preconception.

What to Do

Spend time with a child or, better yet, a group of children, under six. Volunteer at a nursery school or kindergarten, find a playgroup, or stop in at the children's area at your health club be sure to get permission). Get down on their level and follow them around for an hour or two. Engage in child's play.

Questions to Ask Yourself in Reflection

- How are children like or dissimilar from adults in their acceptance of one another?
- What is the role of surprise and wonder in their play?
- How do children approach the creation of something new in their lives? How does this compare with your experience?
- What preconceptions did you bring that got in the way of being in beginner's mind?

EXERCISE 2: IDEATION

Materials needed: large sticky notes or paper and pen or pencil, for each individual; flipchart, marking pens, tape.

The next time you need to make a decision about something you're ambivalent about, invite at least two other people to engage in an ideation process to help you create an outcome that you cannot determine on your own. Choose people whom you trust, but who may hold divergent or different points of view from you.

1. Begin by stating the protocols or agreements of your time together.
2. Next, a brief Stringing of the Beads will ground or transition people to being prepared to participate in a meaningful way.
3. State your vision, purpose, core idea, or challenge to be considered. Clarify as needed until everyone understands it.
4. Explore, brainstorm:
   a. Have everyone, including yourself, individually record his or her ideas, solutions, and/or options in silence (up to 10 each).
   b. Taking turns, invite each person to read one idea per turn, including yourself. Ask everyone to just listen without commenting. As the idea is spoken, instruct the speaker to post it on a wall or flipchart sheet.
   c. Continue having each person speak until all ideas are spoken.
   d. Listen for and note common themes or alignment, or what brings energy to the group. Allow for clarifying questions from the group.
5. Synthesis #1: arrange the ideas by theme. Combine duplicate ideas.
   a. Based on this sorting, pick the three or four most popular categories in the group.
   b. Invite everyone to write a second round of ideas by restating, honing, or creating new ideas for these categories.
   c. Have everyone read what they have written again, one by one, placing the idea, observation, or reflection on the wall by the related category. Allow for clarifying questions and further observations.

6. Synthesis #2: consolidate into one or two primary themes.
   a. Reflect back what you have noticed is common among all of you and where the group's energy is focused.
   b. Thank the participants for their engagement and creativity.

Journaling Questions

Imagine a time in your practice or life when you experienced the alignment of a group. Did you create something new?

- How did distraction (in the form of dissent, inertia, fear, or messiness) manifest, and how was it overcome (or not)?
- As a Convener, how did you respond, or not respond, to the situation?
- Out of this, what was cocreated? Where did the desire for cocreation override the fear and allow for unexpected and unimagined results?

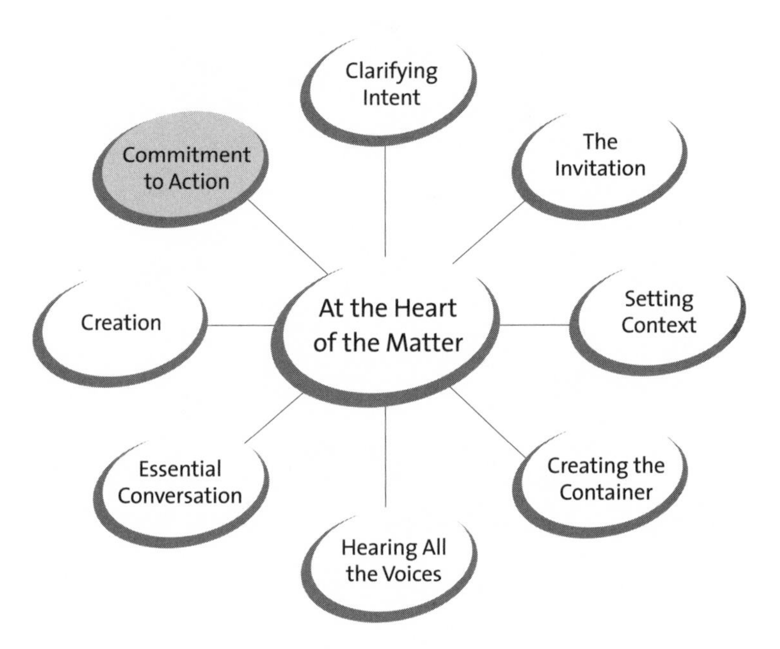
Clarifying Intent
The Invitation
Setting Context
Creating the Container
Hearing All the Voices
Essential Conversation
Creation
Commitment to Action
At the Heart of the Matter

9. COMMITMENT TO ACTION

An individual and/or collective agreement to be responsible and accountable for the way forward

WHY DO WE NEED *COMMITMENT TO ACTION*?

For the harvest of our creation to be of value, we are compelled to take *committed action*. Without commitment, the creation that has emerged from our time together may be lost or greatly diminished.

This final Aspect of the Convening Wheel generates new circumstances and situations that may well offer opportunities for further relationships. Since we are working with a wheel rather than a linear model, finding ourselves at the last Aspect does not bring us to the end. In fact, we may find ourselves returning again and again to the Convening Wheel as a resource as we navigate the meetings, gatherings, and conversations of our lives. Like the wheel, the human experience is more a continuing journey than a destination.

Commitment to Action may take many forms. It can be a decision to do something or a decision to do nothing. It can be one person agreeing to be accountable or many people agreeing to be accountable—individually or as a collective whole. It can be shared, or it can be private. More than a casual item on a to-do list, the *Commitment to Action* could be a question we commit to asking ourselves or a determined stake in the ground.

As Conveners, we guide ourselves and the group through an internal and external journey so that we are all prepared for authentic engagement, where crucial connection and trust can be achieved. We then tend and nurture the *Creation* of something new that emerges from the group, which leads to the possibility and promise of *Commitment to Action*. Learning how to have committed action that develops through alignment is the gift of our authentic engagement, is effective, and is deeply satisfying. True buy-in, true understanding, and focused energy are the byproducts of our time together, and committed action will bring this energy into the future.

CHALLENGE

Absence of alignment

Have we aligned ourselves with the way forward? If commitment is a product of alignment, we must stay alert for what has been created that is new, is worthwhile, and has the highest potential for alignment within the group. We look for surprises and breakthroughs, and for something new that is energizing to us and to the rest of the group. Again, we intervene and/or regroup if we discern a break in authentic engagement or if something is still missing that the group needs in order to be aligned.

The creative process for the Convener can be a time of letting go and letting come, as well as a time to move things along. In its most elegant form, moving from creativity to commitment can be an effortless natural flow that seems logical and apparent to all participants, based on the seamless unfolding of the convening process. We may also encounter resistance, pushback, and conflict.

while we wait for the celebration
that will burst forth when
the world is set aright
perhaps it would be good and wise
to set a place at today's table
where those who will do the work
can be fed
and
since we are those people
perhaps right here
around these sturdy tables
and glowing campfires
and sacred spaces
and living rooms everywhere
right now is a good time
to engage in conversations that matter
to speak of possibilities
to give language to our hopes
and with our words
to begin to BE THE CHANGE
we wish to see

—*Minx Boren*[1]

During this phase, we may very well experience the greatest expression of movement and energy. As the close of the meeting is upon us, there is a natural tendency to want to come to a conclusion or wrap things up in a tidy bow. We've spent our time together for a purpose, and the desire for action may be the driving force now.

Our encouragement and support for the creative process is crucial. As the Conveners, we keep our eyes and ears open for dissent and inertia while allowing for chaos as well as order.

> CREATION TOWARD *our highest potential goes beyond knowledge to deeper wisdom and intelligence from the well of the connected community. Commitment to action builds easily as appreciation of the process and the product inspires a desire for manifestation.*
>
> —*Myron Lowe*[2]

Engagement and a sense of discovery within the community are held as necessary components of completion.

PRINCIPLE

Shared actions and behaviors create movement toward a common future of consequence and accountability.

We've come to this point, at the close of our gathering, having traveled a path around the Convening Wheel. If all has gone well, there is an understanding among the participants of what is needed. Meaningful action comes through the alignment of the group with something new for which we all are willing to share responsibility.

The participants in our gathering enter *Commitment to Action* because we want consequence as a result of our gathering. As the Conveners, we find the new that has emerged in alignment within the group, and we ask the participants to be accountable to bring that new into a shared future. Making a *Commitment to Action* that is inspired through an alignment with others, because we have authentically engaged, is effective and deeply satisfying.

ESSENTIAL QUESTIONS

What is needed to allow for the highest level of commitment, responsibility, and accountability?

What is already occurring or has been put into action?

What actions will I take that will make it more likely that people will act?

We ask ourselves what we have been noticing that others may have not. There is no set form for the action to take; however, as Conveners, we are in a position to determine what is needed at this time and declare or invite action. We design the form of the *Commitment to Action* to capitalize on the alignment of those present toward a common way forward.

During this Aspect, it is vital to determine what will be the method of bringing to light the *Commitment to Action* from the participants. The commitment can be verbal, written, collective, or individual. It can be undisclosed or shared. The responsibility of the Convener is not to hold the participants accountable or for the participants to hold each other accountable. The Convener is the conduit or facilitator of the process, and his or her role is to hold the possibility for alignment and *Commitment to Action*.

If true commitment is to come forth, the participants will all hold themselves accountable. This kind of *Commitment to Action*, where people are truly responsible and accountable for their future, cannot be achieved by coercion, motivation, or manipulation.

MAKING IT REAL

The design for purposeful action is embedded in the collective wisdom of the group and in the energy generated toward a common shared future that all can see and agree upon. Our journey around the Convening Wheel has brought us to this moment of decision, a place of firmly taking a stand. As Conveners, we want to be clear within ourselves that our foundational purpose and intent are reflected in the outcome to which we are now willing to be responsible, accountable, and committed. Have we inwardly and collectively come to resonance and integrity, so that the *Commitment to Action* that each is willing to take will reflect the alignment of the group?

This is a good time to determine the level of commitment needed and desired. Honoring different stages of readiness fosters individual empowerment and collective action. The Convener is now paying close attention to where the determination of the group is most alive and in what areas the group is most willing and able to make a commitment to move forward.

GOOD WILL FINDING

A major manufacturing company had merged with another organization. Each of the two human resources (HR) departments had its own culture and way of doing things, and a seemingly irresolvable conflict had arisen. A three-day offsite retreat was called to bring the two departments together to develop a common human resources strategy for the whole organization. Craig was asked to convene.

He knew that the group had to experience a "We're all in this together" attitude in order to achieve the objective of the retreat. He used the power of the Convening Wheel to engage the participants. For two days, the group practiced the Art of Convening methods, and achieved and maintained authentic engagement. At times, passions ran high, and at others, the atmosphere was thick with frustration. Craig's challenge was to maintain a high level of involvement by continually reinforcing the protocols and bringing the conversation back to *Hearing All the Voices*. The participants' habitual tendencies to multitask, along with the differing and conflicting personalities, kept Craig focused on his intent while simultaneously slowing the pace and deepening the conversation.

Neither Craig nor anyone else knew what the outcome would be and how it would be carried into the larger organization, but he had faith that the group members would determine that for themselves.

On the last day, however, when it looked as if there might be a mandated command-and-control outcome during an open discussion with the full circle of participants, the answer came. The HR director of the parent organization offered that she and her team had learned a great deal from the other HR team during the two days, and were ready to begin collaboration on the creation of new principles and strategies that would be consistent with the common values and behaviors they had been able to identify through the weekend of open—and often charged—discussion.

She said she was prepared to make a personal commitment to work together in good faith, acknowledging that there would be disagreements ahead and their work had just begun.

Knowing that creation had taken place and the moment for a collective commitment to action was at hand, Craig requested a moment of silence for everyone to reflect on the offer and commitment that had just been made. He then asked the participants to speak to how they felt at the moment. Not necessarily about what she had said, but how they were feeling at that moment about the process.

The energy in the room was electric with possibility.

One by one, as each spoke in turn around the circle, the participants said how good it felt to be asked about what they thought and then to be heard! Quite spontaneously, each then spoke of his or her commitment to help make the new principles and strategies a reality.

The power of hearing these voices was indeed an Arc of Recognition. It was the recognition that they were now one group. They had become aligned and committed to a way forward together.[3]

If we are still struggling with a group, then we accept that what is new may need further work to bring alignment with it. We may decide to return to a previous Aspect to bring us and the group to congruence, or ask for the *Commitment to Action* to be the commitment of the participants to continue their work together in a new way or with a new spirit of good will. It is still an important *Commitment to Action,* even out of our disagreement, to be accountable to continue to show up—as long as we are not just postponing.

REFRAMING COMMITMENT

The commitment phase of most meetings is often associated with pressure and performance. A reframing of the concept of commitment may be helpful. Instead of thinking of another thing to add to our (and others') already-packed to-do lists, we might ask the group to consider these questions as a form of commitment:

- What is my stake in the ground for the next 30 days?
- What is something that stretches me, creating new learnings and growth?
- What is something that creates value for myself and/or my group?

Heartland makes use of two effective practices, each getting at bringing *Commitment to Action* in different ways. Commitment Statements and the Commitment Cards process are used at the close of most of our meetings and gatherings.

The Commitment Statement is a powerful tool for bringing focus and closure to any group meeting, regardless of the content or meeting methodology employed. Simply invite each person to speak briefly about a specific commitment he or she is willing to make. We normally use the Stringing the Beads practice of allowing each person to speak in turn without interruption. In this case, the art is in the formation of the right question for that group.

Here are a few sample questions that may get at a few popular issues:

- "Based on what we know is needed to execute/complete this project/strategy, what is a commitment you are willing to actualize toward its success in the next __ days?" (Unless something needs to be completed immediately, 30 days is often a useful time frame that allows for an idea or strategy to develop and be implemented.)
- "What is a commitment you are willing to make in the next 30 days to enhance the esprit de corps of your team at least twofold?"

The Commitment Card process has become a popular feature at each Thought Leader Gathering. Prior to closing the final Stringing of the Beads, we pass out blank Commitment Cards and envelopes. The intention is to build cognitive commitment and to reinforce the muscle of commitment by having participants write a commitment to themselves. The question often is, "What is a commitment, in my life and/or work, that I'm willing to actualize in the next 30 days?"

A COMMITMENT TO COURAGE

In times of change (whether perceived positively or negatively), it's critical that team members are empowered, embrace their role as change leaders, and understand that they have control over their own actions, which have an impact on and influence our culture/environment. This is one of the greatest takeaways from the Art of Convening training.

The AoC also provides an opportunity to connect with my colleagues and peers so that I feel like part of a larger community—like we are all in this together; they provide a safe space to share and reflect (something we frequently miss out on during the chaos); and they provide tools and skills that support my personal development, which I can apply in our business environment.

I have learned a tremendous amount about *listening* and how to have productive, meaningful conversations. As a communications professional, I would have thought I was better at this naturally. I attribute much of the positive change in my attitude, perspective, and approach to learnings from this training and our dialogue in general.

In return, my commitment to you is to have courage, to lead the way, to embrace and effect change. Thank you for empowering and equipping me to do so.

—*By Lauren Kettner*[4]

As Conveners, we will continue to learn, hone, and develop each Aspect of the Convening Wheel for our next gatherings, knowing that authentic engagement creates a foundation of form and function; meaningful experiences; and breakthrough, transformational outcomes.

WHERE WE ARE ON THE CONVENING WHEEL

1. *At the Heart of the Matter*—We have explored who we are and how we will be in relationship with others.
2. *Clarifying Intent*—We have identified an intention consistent with *At the Heart of the Matter* that has substance and is acted upon.
3. *The Invitation*—We have extended a sincere invitation with genuine hospitality, generosity, and conviction.
4. *Setting Context*—We have clearly communicated the form, function, and purpose of our gathering.
5. *Creating the Container*—We have prepared a physical space with beauty and life, and we have agreed on terms of engagement or protocols that bring safety for our time together.
6. *Hearing All the Voices*—We have spoken and heard every other person speak in our gathering, creating an authentic whole.
7. *Essential Conversation*—We have entered into a meaningful exchange in an atmosphere of trust.
8. *Creation*—We have observed and nurtured the emergence of something new in our gathering.
9. *Commitment to Action*—We have concluded the gathering with an individual and/or collective commitment to be responsible and accountable for the way forward.

Commitment to Action is the final Aspect of the Convening Wheel. However, as in all circles, the end brings us to the beginning, *At the Heart of the Matter*, the hub of the Convening Wheel that has informed and supported us throughout this journey.

Things to Remember

Challenge: *Absence of alignment.* Have we aligned ourselves with the way forward?

Principle: *Shared actions and behaviors create movement toward a shared future of consequence and accountability.*

Essential Questions:

- What is needed to allow for the highest level of commitment, responsibility, and accountability?
- What is *already* occurring or has been put into action?
- What actions will I take that may encourage others to act?

Aspect-Strengthening Exercises

Checklist for the Gathering at Hand

- Do I know what commitment means to me?
- Do I know what methods or processes I will draw upon to enable the group to take collective or individual action?

EXERCISE 1: REFLECTIVE QUESTIONS

Answer these questions to build the experience of commitment:

- What is my role in creating change?
- What do I say I will do, and how do I hold myself accountable?
- Recalling the commitments I have in my life, what do they mean to me?

EXERCISE 2: PRACTICE REFRAMING COMMITMENT

Reframe commitments from "another thing to add to the to-do" list, to the following:

- What is my stake in the ground for the next 30 days?
- What is something that stretches me, creating new learnings and growth?

- What is something that creates value for myself and/or my group?

Brainstorm other ways to make a commitment that are reasonably meaningful and doable even for people with packed schedules and to-do lists.

EXERCISE 3: 10X COMMITMENT

Our friend Bill Veltrop, of Pathfinders and the Monterey Institute for Social Architecture, developed the "10X Commitment" mindset and practice. Use this practice as an exercise for developing your capacity for commitment.

10X Commitment

Knowing that what we *aspire to* can be more significant and motivating than what we can *easily achieve*, think of a commitment you have made or want to make to do or accomplish something meaningful to you—personally, socially, or practically. Now, mentally multiply that commitment by 10. That is your 10X Commitment.

Your 10X Commitment should feel impossible. That's the point. By aspiring to something that seems unattainable, we establish conviction and motivation that could last a lifetime. It is a generative mindset that can bring more vivid wonder to our lives than we could ever predict.

Tips for Working with 10X Commitments

- Think of your 10X Commitment(s) as an ongoing, ever-evolving process—more a state of mind than a specific goal, more a privilege than a grudging duty.
- Provide for a *long* gestation period (some experience it as a lifelong process).
- Find or create ongoing groups where the 10X Commitment is or can be a core design element. *We are not intended to do this alone.*
- Within these groups, design for the ongoing sharing of stories of our ever-evolving relationships with our respective 10X Commitments.

- Develop an appreciative, service-centric mindset. Look for and expect to discover the extraordinary in self and others.

EXERCISE 4: 30-DAY COMMITMENT

As practice, next time you meet in a group and you sense an alignment around something new, try out this method of 30-Day Commitment Statements:

- Ask a focusing question for reflection: "From what I know is needed to support the gathering today, what is a commitment I'm willing to make for the next 30 days?"
- Next, ask each person to speak his or her commitment.
- Optionally, give the participants an index card so that they can write down their commitment to take with them when they leave the meeting or gathering.

Journaling Questions

- Has there been a time in your life or practice when you had the experience of a group's total alignment, commitment, and accountability to the collective outcomes of a meeting or engagement?
- What challenges—inertia, distractions, pressing commitments, or overwhelming activities—did you have to overcome in the creative process to reach a true commitment to action? Did you overcome them?
- What are some ways you can think of now to overcome these challenges?

OUR INVITATION

We invite you to join us in the creation of a new time, born in each moment and lived in the fullness of each authentic engagement.

The Guest House

This being human is a guest house.
Every morning a new arrival.

A joy, a depression, a meanness,
some momentary awareness comes
as an unexpected visitor.

Welcome and entertain them all!
Even if they're a crowd of sorrows,
who violently sweep your house
empty of its furniture.

Still treat each guest honourably.
He may be clearing you
out for some new delight.

The dark thought, the shame, the malice,
meet them at the door laughing
and invite them in.

Be grateful for whoever comes,
because each has been sent
as a guide from beyond.

—*Jalal al-Din Rumi*[1]

Heartland and the Art of Convening are integrally connected to a worldwide web of individuals and organizations actively creating a global renaissance of thought and behavior, based on restoring wholeness to ourselves, our communities, our organizations, and the world. Some are referenced in this book in the "People Doing Good Things" and "Acknowledgments and Gratitude" sections.

This notion of *restoring wholeness* is recognizable by an absence of fear and a generosity of spirit. When we, as Conveners, tap into the generosity inherent in people, the wealth of knowledge and wisdom in any gathering is revealed. That wisdom is felt as a connection to being whole, both individually and collectively.

When we feel and experience wholeness, our connection to one another and the world around us becomes less hostile and more inviting.

There is a river flowing now very fast.
It is so great and swift that there are those who will be afraid.
They will try to hold on to the shore.
They will feel they are being torn apart and they will suffer greatly.
Know the river has its destination.
The elders say we must let go of the shore, and push off and into the river,
keep our eyes open, and our head above the water.
See who is in there with you and celebrate.

—*Excerpted from* The Hopi Elders' Prophecy[2]

As the Hopi Elders prophesied, the river of life is flowing fast, and many around us will be afraid. As the gatherers and holders of the people, we keep our hearts and eyes open to those who are with us and celebrate.

This is an invitation to become the "guest house" for the possibility that all those who walk through your door are whole and perfect just as they are, that each interaction with another human being is an opportunity for authentic relationship, and that a transformation occurs in that interaction.

This is a good time to be alive. Stay in touch.

—Craig, Patricia, and Cindy

ARROWS FOR YOUR QUIVER

Resources We May Draw On, in Our Work as Conveners

ARROW 1: STRINGING THE BEADS

Speaking and Listening in the Presence of the Sacred

By Pele Rouge Chadima

The way we speak and listen to our self and others determines the way we experience our world.

Stringing the Beads is an ancient, indigenous human practice founded upon two fundamental premises:

- That all of life is sacred;
- And that all of our voices are important, and for there to be wholeness and balance, each voice must be heard, each must be respected—each has wisdom to share.

Creating a space for both the presence of the sacred and the hearing of all voices is the essence of Stringing the Beads.

Stringing the Beads is a way of awakening the field of relationship that connects us all. It is a way of accessing and allowing the unique wisdom, power, and opportunity present in each moment to emerge.

The practice of Stringing the Beads grew out of the time when we were all tribal people, living in close proximity to one another and to the earth. Although practiced in different ways and by different names in different cultures, Stringing the Beads was fundamental to the strength and well-being of the people and the community in which they lived.

It is no less essential or vital today.

The Metaphor of Stringing the Beads

Imagine a timelessly beautiful necklace made of exquisite beads, each bead unique, each bead contributing in an essential way to the overall beauty and power of the necklace.

And now imagine that *you* are one of those beads—uniquely magnificent, full of genius and mystery. And imagine that you are sitting in a circle with others, equally unique, equally wise.

Slowly, by passing a talking piece clockwise around the circle as the words of each person are spoken, we create a thread of connection that transforms us from independently beautiful "beads" to a necklace of unimagined possibility, wisdom, and strength.

Stringing the Beads is the act and art of gathering all of the beads to make a whole strong, powerful, and beautiful necklace—never the same and yet always more than the sum of all the individual beads.

We String the Beads by inviting each person to speak from the heart to the others in the circle and then listening deeply from the heart as others speak, one by one, until all who wish to speak are heard. This practice allows a deeper wisdom to emerge from the group than is possible to predict.

It allows us, once again, to experience our deep connection to one another—to experience our differences as gifts that create the possibility of greater wisdom and strength, rather than as more reasons to separate.

It reminds us of the best of who we are—as individuals and as a people whose lives matter. It carries us home, to ourselves, to one another, and to the web of life in which we live out our individual and collective lives.

ARROW 2: WISDOM CIRCLES

Evoking the Wisdom of the Group

Wisdom Circles are an effective and efficient way for any small-group breakout session to get to the heart of the matter in any gathering.

Getting Started

- Pull chairs into a circle with no table in the middle.
- Use a *talking piece* to pass if you wish.
- Begin by Stringing the Beads. Each person takes one to two minutes to address a pre-determined question or theme.
- Each person speaks in turn moving clockwise around the circle.
- Do a second round; or, open the circle for insights and reflections.

Wisdom Circle Etiquette *(things to keep in mind)*

- It's helpful to listen and ask questions versus giving advice or "the answer."
- Notice the difference between advice (talking at) and wisdom (being spoken through).
- Speak only if you wish; you may pass at any time.
- Listen deeply for the wisdom that is emerging.
- Allow a pause between each person speaking.

PRINCIPLES OF CONVERSATION

Listen

. . . with respect for all the voices.

. . . without fixing, problem-solving, advice-giving.

Speak from Your Own Experience

Speak from the "I," from your own experience.

What is on your mind/heart?

Slow Down the Conversation

Allow pauses between speakers.

Suspend Certainty

Notice your assumptions.

Look for the surprises.

Allow Space for Difference

Be aware of your judgments.

Honor the questions and the inquiry.

. . . and, you can always take back what you said.

ARROW 3: A CONVENING WHEEL SUMMARY

Putting It All Together

At the Heart of the Matter
Who I am in relationship with others

Challenge	Principle	Essential Questions
Staying connected Do we choose to open ourselves to relationship or do we choose to close?	Knowing who I am allows me to be in authentic engagement.	Who am I as a human being? How will I be in relationship with others?

Clarifying Intent
The alignment of our intention with the purpose of our engagement

Challenge	Principle	Essential Questions
Doubt	Our intent has substance that is acted upon.	What are my intentions? Are they in line with who I am? Who are we to be together?

The Invitation
A sincere offering to engage that integrates purpose and intent

Challenge	Principle	Essential Questions
Rejection	The combination of sincerity, hospitality, and generosity is a strong attractor for full presence.	Who am I to invite? What is at the heart of my invitation? Why should they come?

Setting Context

Communicating the form, function, and purpose of our engagement and intent

Challenge	Principle	Essential Questions
Assumption is the challenge Assume and doom	The clear articulation of purpose and intent allows the highest potential for the actualization of that purpose.	What is this gathering about? What do the participants need to know to show up ready to fully participate? What is our individual and collective purpose for this engagement, and for the sake of what do we do this work?

Creating the Container

Creating the physical and energetic field within which we meet

Challenge	Principle	Essential Questions
Reluctance to impose our will on others	Clear and accepted boundaries integrated with an enlivened environment allow safety and openness.	What is needed for the participants to feel safe in this gathering? What will enliven the environment? What protocols and agreements must be present?

Hearing All the Voices

When each person speaks, is heard and is present and accounted for

Challenge	Principle	Essential Questions
Impatience/ judgment	Each voice is needed to reveal the authentic wisdom in our engagement.	Who are we and what have we come to say and do together? How will we hear all the voices at this gathering? What methods and practices will allow for the full expression of all participants?

Essential Conversation

Meaningful exchange within an atmosphere of trust

Challenge	Principle	Essential Questions
Self-consciousness	Meaningful exchange creates a connected and interdependent whole.	Has the ground been adequately laid for essential conversation to occur? What am I now aware of or open to (that perhaps I was not before)? What wisdom is already present?

Creation

Something new that emerges from engagements of shared purpose and trust

Challenge	Principle	Essential Questions
Disengagement	The emergence of something new that did not exist before is the root of innovation and meaningful contribution.	What are we to create together? How will I recognize and harvest the wisdom being created? What is the new that we can bring back to our relationships and communities, personal and organizational?

Commitment to Action

An individual and/or collective agreement to be responsible and accountable for the way forward

Challenge	Principle	Essential Questions
Absence of alignment	Shared actions and behaviors create movement toward a common future of consequence and accountability.	What is needed to allow for the highest level of commitment, responsibility, and accountability? What is already occurring or has been put into action? What actions will I take that will make it more likely that people will act?

NOTES

Introduction

1. Peter Block, "Leading Is Convening," *Perdido* 15, no. 2 (2008).
2. *Facilitation* definition from *Encarta*, http://encarta.msn.com/encnet/features/dictionary/DictionaryResults.aspx?lextype=3&search=facilitation.

Chapter 1. At the Heart of the Matter

1. Minx Boren, poem ©2009; written expressly for this book. From the heart, mind, and pen of Minx Boren, author of *Feeling My Way—99 Poetic Journeys* (Palm Beach Gardens, FL: Coach Minx Inc., 2008). This and other works by Minx Boren can be found at www.coachminx.com/poetry/books.html.
2. Terry Chapman, "Forging the Inner Heart"; written while engaged in the Art of Convening course, expressly as a contribution to this book, http://sabbathjourney.typepad.com.
3. Michael Bush, CEO, Whalen Co.; extemporaneous remark at the November 1999 Thought Leader Gathering, Menlo Park, CA.
4. Thanks to Terry Chapman.
5. Adapted from HeartMath, LLC, Heart Empowerment Workshop.
6. Thanks to Terry Chapman. Abraham Heschel quote from *The Sabbath* (New York: Farrar, Straus and Giroux, 2005), 17.

Chapter 2. Clarifying Intent

1. Thomas J. Hurley, "Archetypal Practices for Collective Wisdom," Collective Wisdom Initiative (2004), www.collectivewisdominitiative.org/papers/hurley_archetypal.htm (accessed May 13, 2010).
2. Pele Rouge Chadima, "Nurturing the Emergence of Collective Wisdom," Collective Wisdom Initiative, www.collectivewisdominitiative.org/papers/pele_nurturing.htm (accessed May 13, 2010).
3. Minx Boren, poem ©2009. From the heart, mind, and pen of Minx Boren, author of *Feeling My Way—99 Poetic Journeys* (Palm Beach Gardens, FL: Coach Minx Inc., 2008). This and other works by Minx Boren can be found at www.coachminx.com/poetry/books.html.
4. Eric Babinet, Salesforce.com; story written expressly as a contribution to this book.

Chapter 3. The Invitation

1. Diarmuid O'Murchu, *Quantum Theology: Spiritual Implications of the New Physics* (New York: Crossroad Publishing Co., 2004).
2. Peter Block, *Community: The Structure of Belonging* (San Francisco: Berrett-Koehler Publishers, 2009), 113.

3. "Inviting Full Presence" is a composite of stories from the field, gleaned from reports by Art of Convening participants. Names of people and organizations have been changed, but the important points of the story are true.
4. Eric Utne, founder, *Utne Reader*; story written expressly as a contribution to this book.
5. Sheila Hines Edmondson, StayWell Health Management; story written expressly as a contribution to this book.

Chapter 4. Setting Context

1. Wilhelm Dilthey, *Introduction to the Human Sciences: An Attempt to Lay a Foundation for the Study of Society and History* (Detroit: Wayne State University Press, 1989).
2. A. R. Ammons, *Tape for the Turn of the Year* (New York: W. W. Norton, 1994).
3. This is our personal adaptation of the Institute of HeartMath®'s Freeze-Frame® technique and has been included by written agreement with the Institute.

Chapter 5. Creating the Container

1. Doc Childre and Howard Martin, *The HeartMath Solution* (New York: HarperOne, 2000).
2. Peter Block, *The Answer to How Is Yes: Acting on What Matters* (San Francisco: Berrett-Koehler Publishers, 2003), 178.
3. Bev Scott, Bev Scott Consulting, author of *Consulting on the Inside* (Alexandria, VA: ASTD Press, 2000) and founder of "The 3rd Act Workshop Series"; written expressly as a contribution to this book.
4. Pele Rouge Chadima, from the online essay, "Nurturing the Emergence of Collective Wisdom," www.collectivewisdominitiative.org/papers/pele_nurturing.htm.
5. Minx Boren, poem ©2009. From the heart, mind, and pen of Minx Boren, author of *Feeling My Way—99 Poetic Journeys* (Palm Beach Gardens, FL: Coach Minx Inc., 2008). This and other works by Minx Boren can be found at www.coachminx.com/poetry/books.html.
6. "The Virtual Campfire" is an abridgment of the account of an actual Art of Convening training session.

Chapter 6. Hearing All the Voices

1. "The Retreat" is a composite of stories from the field gleaned from reports by Art of Convening participants. Names of people and/or organizations have been changed, but the important points of the story are true.
2. Otto Scharmer, Peter Senge, Frank Jaworski and Betty Sue Flowers, *Presence: Human Purpose and the Field of the Future* (San Francisco: Berrett-Koehler Publishers, 2004), 11.

3. Sue Patton Thoele, *The Woman's Book of Courage: Meditations for Empowerment and Peace of Mind* (Newburyport, MA: Conari, 2003).
4. "A Joyful Hearing" is a composite of stories from the field gleaned from reports by Art of Convening participants. Names of people and/or organizations are changed, but the important points of the story are true.
5. Paul G. Ward, transformation consultant and life coach; story written expressly as a contribution to this book.
6. Stringing the Beads as a practice is the subject of a forthcoming book by Pele Rouge Chadima, *Resonance* (www.resonance.to). A full explanation of Stringing the Beads is included in "Arrows for Your Quiver." Although this practice is found in many cultures, it is most known by name in indigenous cultures. The form that we adapted here was passed on to us by Pele Rouge and FireHawk, teachers of the Delicate Lodge tradition.

Chapter 7. Essential Conversation

1. "Extrovert/Introvert Dilemma" was adapted from a story relayed by Pam Hull, HealthEast Care System.
2. Anne Griswold; written expressly as a contribution to this book, at the conclusion of an Art of Convening training conducted for LifeScan Corporation.
3. Lauren Patterson, Service-Learning Initiative of Southwest Colorado; story written expressly as a contribution to this book.

Chapter 8. Creation

1. Brenda Ueland, *Strength to Your Sword Arm: Selected Writings* (Duluth, MN: Holy Cow! Press, 1996).
2. Elizabeth Becker, Becker & Company; written expressly as a contribution to this book.

Chapter 9. Commitment to Action

1. Minx Boren, poem ©2009. From the heart, mind, and pen of Minx Boren, author of *Feeling My Way—99 Poetic Journeys* (Palm Beach Gardens, FL: Coach Minx Inc., 2008). This and other works by Minx Boren can be found at www.coachminx.com/poetry/books.html.
2. Myron Lowe, IT Director, University of Minnesota; written expressly as a contribution to this book.
3. "Good Will Finding" is a composite of stories from the field gleaned from reports by Art of Convening participants and Craig's personal experience. Names of people and/or organizations are changed, but the important points of the story are true.
4. "A Commitment to Courage," by Lauren Kettner, employee communications specialist, LifeScan, Inc.; story written expressly as a contribution to this book.

Our Invitation

1. Jalal al-Din Rumi, *The Essential Rumi,* trans. Coleman Barks (New York: HarperOne, 1997).
2. Hopi Elders' Prophecy; Oraibi, Arizona; June 8, 2000.

GLOSSARY

Although the following terms may have other, more common uses, the definitions offered here represent the ways in which these terms are used in this book. Each definition could be prefaced with, "As used in *The Art of Convening.*"

accountability. State of taking responsibility for oneself to remain consistent and in alignment with a value, action, presence, or intention.

Arc of Recognition. The phenomenon of each participant in a gathering seeing and accepting all of the other participants for who they really are, while simultaneously being seen and accepted for who you really are.

Aspect. Any one of the nine parts of the Convening Wheel.

At the Heart of the Matter. Who I am in relationship with others, and why we engage.

authority. Not power over, but "authoring" one's life.

calling. The overarching passion for a particular vocation, avocation, or activity.

challenge. The fundamental barrier that must be seen in order to continue to the next Aspect of the Convening Wheel.

Clarifying Intent. The alignment of our intention with the purpose of our engagement.

coherence. To become aligned in principles, relationships, or interests; to be logically and aesthetically consistent.

Commitment to Action. An individual and/or collective agreement to be responsible and accountable for the way forward.

container. An energetic and/or physical space where people gather.

convening. Gathering and holding people for the sake of authentic engagement.

Convening Wheel. Model of the Art of Convening method, consisting of a circle whose center Aspect (part) is surrounded by eight additional Aspects.

core elements. For each of the nine Aspects of the Convening Wheel, the Challenge, Principle, and Essential Questions.

Creating the Container. Creating the physical and energetic field within which we meet.

Creation. Something new that emerges from engagements of shared purpose and trust.

energetic field (also called *energetic container*). The "inner container," consisting of protocols and rules of engagement, that defines and provides boundaries for a gathering.

essence. The core of who we are and how we are in relationship with others; an internally sound, strong characteristic of ourselves that permeates our meeting or gathering.

Essential Conversation. Meaningful exchange within an atmosphere of trust.

facilitation. The process of making something easy or easier.

field. Space within which we gather. (See *energetic field*.)

gathering. Group of two or more people called together for a purpose.

genesis. Source or beginning—*genesis story* refers to a history of the origin of something.

Hearing All the Voices. Each person speaks, is heard, and is present and accounted for.

hold. Commit to be with, in a genuine way, while evoking the highest presence from and providing safety for (as in "*hold* the people").

intention. The result we desire our actions, words, or presence to bring.

Invitation, The. A sincere offering to engage that integrates purpose and intent.

journal keeping. Writing about personal thoughts or experiences; not just a diary or documentation but a practice of listening.

presence. The condition of being fully alert, aware, and attentive to one's current place, company, and surroundings.

purpose. When used generally: the full reason for something; when used to refer to the Convener: who the Convener is and how the Convener will be in relationship with others.

resonance. A condition of understanding and feeling connected to a thing, thought, or idea.

Setting Context. Communicating the form, function, and purpose of our engagement and intent.

Stringing the Beads. Method for *Hearing All the Voices* that uses the metaphor of people as unique beads and the visualization of running a string through each as he or she speaks, thus creating a whole.

transformation. A fundamental and lasting shift in thinking, feeling, or understanding that has a tangible effect on one's quality of life.

transition. The space between activities. In a gathering, the time when people are asked to shift or move themselves, physically, mentally, or spiritually.

Transition Exercise. May be a poem, meditation, visualization, stretching of arms or legs, or brief breathing exercise that helps people to re-center, recalibrate, and be more fully present for what comes next.

SUGGESTED READING

Baldwin, Christina. *Calling the Circle: The First and Future Culture.* Columbus, NC: Swan Raven, 1994.

Baldwin, Christina, and Ann Linnea. *The Circle Way: A Leader in Every Chair.* San Francisco: Berrett-Koehler, 2010.

Barnes, Peter. *Capitalism 3.0: A Guide to Reclaiming the Commons.* San Francisco: Berrett-Koehler, 2006.

Barrett, Richard. *Building a Values-Driven Organization: A Whole System Approach to Cultural Transformation.* Burlington, MA: Butterworth-Heinemann/Elsevier, 2006.

Block, Peter. *The Answer to How Is Yes: Acting on What Matters.* San Francisco: Berrett-Koehler, 2003.

———. *Community: The Structure of Belonging.* San Francisco: Berrett-Koehler, 2008.

Bohm, David. *Wholeness and the Implicate Order.* New York: Routledge, 1980.

Boren, Minx. *Ripe: A Collection of Passionate Poetry and Pears.* Xlibris, 2005.

———. *Feeling My Way—99 Poetic Journeys.* www.CoachMinx.com/poetry/books.html, 2008.

Briskin, Alan, et al. *The Power of Collective Wisdom: And the Trap of Collective Folly.* San Francisco: Berrett-Koehler, 2009.

Brown, Juanita, David Isaacs, and the World Café Community. *The World Café: Shaping Our Futures Through Conversations That Matter.* San Francisco: Berrett-Koehler, 2005.

Cooperrider, David L., and Diana Whitney. *Appreciative Inquiry: A Positive Revolution in Change.* San Francisco: Berrett-Koehler, 2005.

Fox, Matthew. *The Reinvention of Work: A New Vision of Livelihood for Our Time.* San Francisco: HarperSanFrancisco, 1994.

Fromm, Erich. *The Art of Loving.* New York: Perennial, 2000.

Holman, Peggy, Tom Devane, and Steven Cady. *The Change Handbook: The Definitive Resource on Today's Best Methods for Engaging Whole Systems.* San Francisco: Berrett-Koehler, 2007.

Jones, Michael. *Artful Leadership: Awakening the Commons of the Imagination.* Bloomington, IN: Trafford, 2006

Kabat-Zinn, Jon. *Mindfulness Meditation: Cultivating the Wisdom of Your Body and Mind.* CD. Niles, IL: Nightingale-Conant, 2002.

Leider, Richard J. *Claiming Your Place at the Fire: Living the Second Half of Your Life on Purpose.* San Francisco: Berrett-Koehler, 2004.

———. *The Power of Purpose: Find Meaning, Live Longer, Better.* San Francisco: Berrett-Koehler, 2010.

Moore Lappé, Frances. *You Have the Power: Choosing Courage in a Culture of Fear.* New York: Tarcher/Penguin, 2005.

O'Donohue, John. *Beauty: The Invisible Embrace.* New York: HarperCollins, 2004.

Owen, Harrison. *Open Space Technology: A User's Guide.* San Francisco: Berrett-Koehler, 2008.

Palmer, Parker J. *A Hidden Wholeness: The Journey Toward an Undivided Life.* San Francisco: Jossey-Bass, 2004.

Perron, Mari, and Dan Odegard. *A Course of Love.* Minneapolis, MN: Itasca Books, 2006.

Ray, Michael. *The Highest Goal: The Secret That Sustains You in Every Moment.* San Francisco: Berrett-Koehler, 2004.

Rechelbacher, Horst M., Ellen Daly, and Victor J. Zurbel. *Alivelihood: The Art of Sustainable Success.* Minneapolis: HMR, 2005.

Renesch, John. *Getting to the Better Future: A Matter of Conscious Choosing.* San Francisco: NewBusinessBooks, 2000.

Scharmer, C. Otto. *Theory U: Leading from the Future as It Emerges.* Cambridge: Society for Organizational Learning, 2007.

Scott, Beverly. *Consulting on the Inside: An Internal Consultant's Guide to Living and Working Inside Organizations.* Alexandria, VA: American Society for Training & Development, 2000.

Senge, Peter, et al. *Presence: Human Purpose and the Field of the Future.* Cambridge: Currency/Doubleday, 2004.

Sibbet, David. *Visual Meetings: How Graphics, Sticky Notes and Idea Mapping Can Transform Group Productivity.* New York: John Wiley & Sons, 2010.

Stanfield, R. Brian, ed. *The Art of Focused Conversation: 100 Ways to Access Group Wisdom in the Workplace.* Gabriola Island, BC, Canada: New Society, 2000.

Tolle, Eckhart. *The Power of Now: A Guide to Spiritual Enlightenment.* Novato, CA: New World Library, 1999.

Wagner, David. *Life as a Daymaker: How to Change the World Simply by Making Someone's Day.* San Diego, CA: Jodere Group, 2003.

Wheatley, Margaret J. *Turning to One Another: Simple Conversations to Restore Hope to the Future.* San Francisco: Berrett-Koehler, 2002.

WindEagle and RainbowHawk. *Heart Seeds: A Message from the Ancestors.* Minneapolis: Beaver's Pond, 2003.

PEOPLE DOING GOOD THINGS

There are outstanding members of the convening community doing great work in the world. We have listed some of them here. Find more details and contact information on our website at http://heartlandcircle.com/peopledoinggood.htm

10TH DOT, VONDA VADEN BATES AND YOGIRAJ CHARLES BATES

10th Dot is pioneering the nexus of personal and collective transformation via whole systems and ancient teachings and practices.

APPRECIATIVE INQUIRY

Appreciative Inquiry involves the art and practice of asking questions that strengthen a system's capacity to apprehend, anticipate, and heighten positive potential.

THE ART OF HOSTING

The Art of Hosting and Convening Conversations That Matter is a powerful leadership practicum as well as a daily pattern and practice for many individuals, communities, families, businesses, and organizations.

DOUG BAKER, SR., SPIRITSEARCH/CONVERSATIONS OF CONSEQUENCE

Doug is a founding Elder of the Heartland community, mentor to many, and community builder. SpiritSearch groups are for leaders who want to examine their spiritual underpinnings as these apply to their life and work.

CHRISTINA BALDWIN AND ANN LINNEA, PEERSPIRIT

PeerSpirit is an educational company that helps facilitate conversation in both business and personal groups with the goal of creating a setting where transformation can occur.

PETER BARNES

Peter stepped forward early in Heartland's story as an investor, counselor, and cheerleader. His generosity in hosting Craig at the Mesa Refuge, a writers' retreat center, was the genesis of this book. He is a cofounder of On the Commons / Common Assets; the originator of the Sky Trust idea; an author; and an expert on the economics of natural resource commons.

RICHARD BARRETT, RICHARD BARRETT & ASSOCIATES LLC, BARRETT VALUES CENTRE

We first met Richard while he was at the World Bank. He was an early board member and confidant in the development of Heartland and then AoC. His work on systemic culture change is being honored by governments and large economic systems on a global level.

THE BERKANA INSTITUTE

Berkana supports life-affirming leaders around the globe. Berkana intentionally supports those who are giving birth to the new forms, processes, and leadership that will restore hope to the future.

PETER BLOCK

Peter's work and writings have been the single most important source of inspiration for the Art of Convening, bar none. His ruminations have been pivotal in how the AoC has matured and found its voice. You know someone's words matter when you find yourself quoting key concepts and meaningful words. Additionally, his books are core texts for our trainings.

ALAN BRISKIN

As a friend for over 40 years and founding member of the Thought Leader Gatherings, Alan has been a source of inspiration as well as motivation for the completion of the book. Cofounder of the Collective Wisdom Initiative, Alan is a consultant, artist, and researcher.

CENTER FOR SPIRITUALITY & HEALING

The University of Minnesota's Center for Spirituality & Healing is a world-renowned resource that enriches health and well-being by providing high-quality interdisciplinary education, conducting rigorous research, and delivering innovative programs that advance integrative health and healing.

PELE ROUGE CHADIMA AND FIREHAWK HULIN, RESONANCE, THE CENTER OF TIMELESS LEADERSHIP

Truly our life partners and wise elders in many of the Heartland communities. Their life calling as teachers of the Earth Wisdom Teachings of the Delicate Lodge has been profoundly influential on our entire body of work with Heartland and the AoC.

CHARTHOUSE LEARNING CORPORATION, JOHN CHRISTENSEN

John was an early and consistent advocate for the Art of Convening.

COLLECTIVE WISDOM INITIATIVE

We believe there exists a field of collective consciousness—often seen and expressed through metaphor—that is real and influential.

THE DAYMAKER MOVEMENT

David Wagner and his company, Juut SalonSpas, embraced the principles and practices of the AoC early on. His book, *Life as a Daymaker*, influenced our thinking on service and gratitude.

HARRISON OWEN, OPEN SPACE TECHNOLOGY

Harrison is an author, consultant, and photographer. For 40 years he has explored the world and himself, seeking the ways and means toward a deeper understanding of who we all are and how we may live productively with meaning and purpose.

HEARTMATH LLC

HeartMath LLC is dedicated to improving health, performance, and well-being at home and in the workplace.

HOLLYHOCK EDUCATIONAL RETREAT CENTRE

As Canada's leading educational retreat center, Hollyhock is a hub of learning and connection that exists to inspire, nourish, and support people who are making the world better.

RICHARD LEIDER, THE INVENTURE GROUP

Richard is one of Heartland's Elders and a dear friend who has seen us through many life and business transitions. Whenever we solicit his wisdom, it's always spot-on and inspired. His books are required reading for the Art of Convening Trainings as well as leaders of any cut. Richard is legendary in the coaching world as one of the fathers of modern coaching.

AMY LENZO, BEAUTY DIALOGUES, CLEAR LIGHT COMMUNICATIONS, WORLD CAFÉ

Amy has been a professional partner and intimate since the beginning of the Heartland journey and well before. Her genius of bringing beauty and love into the electronic virtual realm is pioneering.

JOEL AND MICHELLE LEVEY, THE INTERNATIONAL CENTER FOR CORPORATE CULTURE & ORGANIZATIONAL HEALTH

The Leveys' company, based in Seattle and Hawaii, is dedicated to developing and renewing organizational cultures in which people flourish, and extraordinary levels of inspired leadership, change resilience, mind fitness, and collective wisdom can thrive.

LIFE SCIENCE FOUNDATION

Using its land and resources, Life Science Foundation exists to create and provide environments for the public that renew, inspire, and enrich all life. Fields of study: Intuition, Integrative Healthcare, New Science, Environment.

NATIONAL COALITION FOR DIALOGUE & DELIBERATION

NCDD brings together those who actively practice, promote, and study inclusive, high-quality conversations. We believe that elevating the quality of thinking and communication in organizations and among citizens is key to solving humanity's most pressing problems.

PARKER PALMER, THE CENTER FOR COURAGE & RENEWAL

Parker's notion of the "shy soul" and popularizing of circles of trust is a huge gift to humanity. It speaks to the soul of convening. His book, *A Hidden Wholeness*, is a text of the AoC Advanced Training and influenced the formation of the Convening Wheel. Parker is founder and senior partner of the Center for Courage & Renewal.

THE PRESENCING INSTITUTE

The Presencing Institute (PI) is a global action research community for profound societal innovation and change. The presencing process is a journey that connects us more deeply both to what wants to emerge in the world and to our emerging, originating self.

MICHAEL RAY

Michael is a trusted advisor and visionary, giving us the support and courage to start the Thought Leader Gatherings in the San Francisco Bay Area and encouraging us along the way to find our voices. His accomplishments are inspiring!

JOHN RENESCH

A longtime visionary in the realm of work and spirit, an active supporter of Heartland and many people and organizations, John is an advisor, mentor, futurist, and writer on matters of social and organizational change.

RUDOLF STEINER FOUNDATION

Rudolf Steiner Foundation creates social benefit through innovative approaches to working with money that reflect the highest aspirations of the human spirit.

OTTO SCHARMER

Otto's influential thinking on Theory U first found a welcome home in the foundational development of the AoC trainings.

DAVID SIBBET, THE GROVE CONSULTANTS INTERNATIONAL

Wise elder, corporate shaman, and charter member of the Thought Leader Gatherings, David is the father of Graphic Facilitation. The Grove is a San Francisco–based consultancy and publisher that offers services and tools to help organizations, teams, and individuals successfully envision and implement change.

SOCIAL VENTURE NETWORK

As 20-year members of SVN, we owe much of the birth of Heartland to many of its members who are visionaries and leaders in "Transforming the Way the World Does Business," the SVN mission.

ERIC UTNE, THE UTNE INSTITUTE

Eric Utne is an entrepreneur, publisher, and educator. In 1984, he founded *Utne Reader*, for which he currently writes a back-page column. Eric has influenced the modern definition of community through the magazine, his groundbreaking books, and the Neighborhood Salon and Community Earth Council movements.

BILL AND MARILYN VELTROP, PATHFINDERS

Bill and Marilyn are the founders of Pathfinders, a seminal personal/ leadership development series. Their work supports pragmatic, visionary leaders in transforming themselves and their organizations in ways that make a lasting difference for all involved.

MARGARET WHEATLEY

Meg was an early friend to Heartland, and her book *Turning to One Another* influenced the design of the Thought Leader Gatherings and early development of the AoC Convening Wheel. She is an internationally acclaimed writer, speaker, and teacher, addressing how we can accomplish our work, sustain our relationships, and willingly step forward to serve in this chaotic time.

WORLD CAFÉ, JUANITA BROWN, DAVID ISAACS

It was on their patio in 1999 that they first sketched out the World Café system to us. We had just started the Thought Leader Gatherings and have become collaborators and thinking partners ever since.

WORLD FOUNDATION FOR THE DISCIPLINE OF PEACE, WINDEAGLE AND RAINBOWHAWK

In this time in which we live, we see the vital need for humanity to take another step toward creating not only peace in each of us, but peace among us.

ACKNOWLEDGMENTS AND GRATITUDE

We shall acknowledge first those whose hands were closest to the crafting of the Art of Convening process, and then the influencers whose heads and hearts offered wisdom, love, and support along the way.

Steve Piersanti, our editor, encouraged us early in the decade to write this book, saying we were the ones to define the territory. His patience over six years is admirable as he masterfully guided us every step of the way.

Craig first became aware of the potential of group transformation at the steps of the Lincoln Memorial on August 26, 1963, during the civil rights March on Washington, and then honed his convening skills at the feet of his parents, Barbara and Earl Neal, during their "thinkers and drinkers" salons throughout his teen years.

Patricia had the inspiration for an AoC book, saying we needed to give the members of the Thought Leader Gatherings the recipe for the unique design and execution of convening the TLGs. It was Peter Barnes who graciously hosted Craig for two weeks at his Mesa Refuge writers' retreat, where the initial outline for the book was created in April 2004.

Pele Rouge Chadima and FireHawk Hulin have been partners on our journey, greatly influencing the Art of Convening and Heartland.

Kate O'Keefe, codesigner of the TLGs and thinking partner over the years, introduced us to the world of group process and design.

We give thanks to the TLG member and conversation starter communities who have been partners in the development and practice field of convening since 1998.

The Art of Convening Training graduates signed on and were willing to create a learning community that deepened the field of convening. Most of the stories, and many of the quotes and poems, come from this community.

A special thank you goes to the AoC Advanced Training groups who helped to further hone the foundation and craft the Convening Wheel over years of collaborative work together. To them we owe much for the content of this book.

The book could not have been written without AoC mentors and trainers Minx Boren, Claudia Eisinger, Paul Strickland and Ann Marie Stuart. Minx helped to sculpt the Wheel and the final edits of the first draft of the manuscript. Claudia, Ann Marie, and Paul have been constant mentors in the development of the trainings and therefore the book.

There are many spiritual, intellectual influences to which we owe much for the core theories and practices of AoC:

Peter Block's unapologetic stakes in the ground about the nature of community and freedom have been inspiring. Richard Leider's deep elder wisdom resonates throughout this book. Meg Wheatley was an early and consistent voice for the power of whole systems in human dynamics. Parker Palmer's personal vulnerability and work with Circles of Trust and Quaker-inspired reflection bring soul to our table. David Bohm's seminal work on dialogue is bedrock. Juanita Brown and David Isaac's deep inquiry into the spiritual realms of human form and interaction manifest in the elegant World Café methodology.

Oscar Ichazo and the Arica Institute introduced Craig and Patricia to the psychospiritual nature of the human condition, while Adi Da taught Craig the radical nature of love. In 1999, Craig was involved in the emergence and publication of the book *A Course of Love*, which serves as a primary source of inspiration.

Amy Lenzo, Eric Utne, Sarah and Paul Strickland, Betsy Stites, John Gisler, and Tom Atchison, have been our dear friends, counselors, and teachers. All along the way, Zoë and Graham François, and Carey and Alec Neal have been a source of love and inspiration to us.

STORY CONTRIBUTORS

Eric Babinet • Elizabeth Becker • Minx Boren • Pele Rouge Chadima • Terry Chapman • Anne Griswold • Sheila Hines Edmondson • Pam Hull • Lauren Kettner • Lauren Patterson • Bev Scott • Ann Marie Stuart • Eric Utne • Bill Veltrop • Paul Ward

POETRY AND QUOTES

A. R. Ammons • Elizabeth Becker • Minx Boren • Peter Block • Michael Bush • Pele Rouge Chadima • Doc Childre and Howard Martin • Wilhelm Dilthey • Albert Einstein • Claudia Eisinger • Hopi Elders • Tom Hurley • Myron Lowe • William Murray • Diarmuid O'Murchu • Jalal al-Din Rumi • Sue Patton Thoele • Brenda Ueland

EDITORS AND REVIEWERS

Tom Atchison • Minx Boren • Sandy Chase • Jeffrey Cufaude • Marisa Handler • Heather Pamula • Steve Piersanti • Amol Ray • Jeevan Sivasubramaniam • Leigh Wilkinson

BERRETT-KOEHLER PRODUCTION STAFF

Book Cover Design, Irene Morris • Copyediting, Elissa Rabellino • Proofreading, Henrietta Bensussen • Indexing, J. Naomi Linzer • Interior Design, Laura Lind • Production, Dianne Platner and Linda Jupiter

PEOPLE WHO HAVE SUPPORTED AND HAD AN IMPACT ON THE CREATION OF THIS BOOK:

Cheryl Alexander Stearns • Anders Axelsson • Tom Atchison • Eric Babinet • Joseph Bailey • Doug Baker Sr. • Katherine Ball • David Banner • Richard Barrett • Vonda Vaden Bates • Yogiraj Charles Bates • Elizabeth Becker • Peter Block • Dan Bohnhorst • Minx Boren • Gail Brinkman • Alan Briskin • Cathy Buelow • Trudy Canine • Pele Rouge Chadima • Terry Chapman • John Christensen • Wallys Conhaim • Martha Coventry • Barbara Davis • Fran Davis • Joe Donofrio • Claudia Eisinger • Cheryl Esposito • Jodie Evans • Mark Finser • Ayn Fox • Graham François • Zoë François • William Frost • Robert Gass • Tom Gegax • Julie Gilbert • John Gillespie • John Gisler • Barbara Greene • Anne Griswold • Willis Harmon • Rebecca Herrero • Jim Higgins • Ned Holle • FireHawk Hulin • Pam Hull • George Johnson • Ellen Kearney • Brian Kempton • Rob Kesselring • Kim Knutson • Susan Kraus • Kimberly Kristenson-Lee • Maureen Lauer • Richard Leider • Amy Lenzo • Ross Levin • Cheri Litsheim • Myron Lowe • Margaret Lulic • Marilyn Mason • Barbara McAfee • Louise Miner • Margaret Mitchell • Wendy Morris • Alec Neal • Barbara Neal • Carey Neal • Deborah Nelson • Kate O'Keefe • Polo and Kiki • Heather Pamula • Debra Paterson • Cheryl Persigehl • Marcia Pillon • Jane Powers • Lynette Raap • Will Raap • Michael Ray • John Renesch • Betsy Sanders • Sandy Sanders • Paul Scheele • Michelle Schmitt • Bev Scott • Jim Secord • Barbara Shipka • David Sibbet • Gary Smaby • Joel Solomon • Jeff Staggs • Nancy Stephan • Paul Strickland • Sarah Strickland • Betsy Stites • Ann Marie Stuart • Marilyn Tam • Bruce Taub • Mark Thompson • Deborah Tompkins • Eric Utne • Nina Rothschild Utne • Vonda Vaden • Bill Veltrop • Marilyn Veltrop • David Wagner • Diana Whitney • Crystal Wold • John Wood

PEOPLE WHO HAVE SIGNIFICANTLY INFLUENCED OUR UNDERSTANDING ABOUT CONVENING:

Tom Atlee • Angeles Arrien • Joseph Bailey • Christina Baldwin • Peter Block • David Bohm • Alan Briskin • Juanita Brown • Pele Rouge Chadima • Doc Chlldre • David Cooperrider

• Adi Da • Stewart Emery • Werner Erhard • Robert Gass • Glenna Gerard • FireHawk Hulin • Tom Hurley • Oscar Ichazo • David Isaacs • Martin Luther King Jr. • Richard Leider • Amy Lenzo • Joel Levey • Michelle Levey • Ann Linnea • Barbara Neal • John O'Donohue • Kate O'Keefe • Harrison Owen • Parker Palmer • Steve Piersanti • Michael Ray • John Renesch • Steve Roberts • Vicki Robin • Otto Scharmer • Peter Senge • David Sibbet • Eric Utne • Bill Veltrop • Marilyn Veltrop • Margaret Wheatley • Diana Whitney • David Whyte • WindEagle and RainbowHawk • Tenneson Woolfe • The Course of Love

THANK YOU TO OUR THOUGHT LEADER GATHERING CONVERSATION STARTERS:

Vickie Abrahamson • Patricia Aburdene • Mark Albion • Angeles Arrien • James Autry • Joseph Bailey • Doug Baker • Peter Barnes • Cathy Barr • Richard Barrett • Vonda Vaden Bates • David Batstone • Barbra Berlovitz • Meredith Beam • Peter Block • Alan Briskin • Peter Brosius • Juanita Brown • Laurie Brown • Tim Brownell • Karen Buckley • Carol Engebretson Byrne • Mary Capozzi • Bob Carlson • Kevin Cashman • Chip Conley • Lori Crever • Sara Criger • Bruce Cryer • Patrick Donovan • Duane Elgin • Stewart Emery • Steve Epp • Chuck Feltz • Dan Ferber • Andrew Ferguson • Stacy Fisher • Margot Fraser • Pablo Gaito • Sandra Gardebring • Tom Gegax • Julie Gilbert • John Gisler • William Gold • Neal Gorenflo • Vincent Gracieux • Mary Hamann-Roland • Dan Hanson • Charlie Hartwell • John Haynes • Barry Heerman • Gay Hendricks • Peter Henschel • Elliot Hoffman • Susan Hubbard • FireHawk Hulin • Pam Hull • Tom Hurley • Ron James • Bob Johansen • Michael Jones • Syl Jones • Eamonn Kelly • Marjorie Kelly • Rick King • Peter Koestenbaum • Joel Kramer • Richard Leider • Doug Lennick • Cyndi Lesher • Ross Levin • Margaret Lulic • Barbara Marx-Hubbard • Marilyn Mason • Deborah Nelson • James O'Dea • David O'Fallon • Karen Oman • Steve Piersanti • Carol Pine • Tad Piper • Miha Pogacnik • Michael Ray • Paul Ray • Horst Rechelbacher • David Reiling • Ocean Robbins • Robert Rosen • Peter Russell • Betsy Sanders • Elizabeth Sahtouris • Otto Scharmer • Laura Scher • John Scherer • Ann Schrader • Julie Schmidt • Rayona Sharpnack • David Sibbet • Gary Smaby •Geoff Sylvester • Betsy Stites • Tom Szaky • Marilyn Tam • Paul Terry • Mark Thompson • Michael Trebony • Yvette Trotman • Nina Rothschild Utne • Peter Vaill • Bill Veltrop • David Wagner • Mal Warwick • Robyn Waters • Barbara Waugh • Margaret Wheatley • Dave Wondra • Daniel Wordsworth • Vivian Wright • Ray Yeh

THANK YOU TO OUR VISIONHOLDERS:
Patricia Aburdene • Mark Albion • Angeles Arrien • James Autry • Chris Avery • Joseph Bailey • David Banner • Peter Barnes • Jane Barrash • Richard Barrett • Peter Block • Juana Bordas • Alan Briskin • Juanita Brown • Rinaldo Brutoco • John Hope Bryant • Victoria Castle • Pele Rouge Chadima • John Christensen • Deidre Combs • Chip Conley • Robert Dickman • Elizabeth Doty • Riane Eisler • Duane Elgin • Tom Gegax • Glenna Gerard • Terry Gips • Marshall Goldsmith • Barry Heerman • Sandy Heierbacher • FireHawk Hulin • Tom Hurley • John Izzo • Maggie Jackson • Bob Johansen • Brian Johnson • George Johnson • Michael Jones • Van Jones • Eamonn Kelly • Fred Kiel • Leo Kim • David Korten • Richard Leider • Joel and Michelle Levey • Stewart Levine • Margaret Lulic • Marilyn Mason • Renee Moorefield • James O'Dea • Kate O'Keefe • Verna Cornelia Price • Kavita Ramdas • Michael Ray • John Renesch • Ann Riley • Peter Russell • Elizabeth Sahtouris • Bernie Saunders • Otto Scharmer • Andrea Batista Schlesinger • Rayona Sharpnack • Sarah Susanka • Marilyn Tam • Mark Thompson • Eric Utne • Leif Utne • Nina Rothschild Utne • Bill Veltrop • David Wagner • Robyn Waters • Diana Whitney • Vivian Wright • Margaret Wheatley

We'd like to thank anyone who has attended a Thought Leader Gathering, participated in an Art of Convening Training, or attended a VisionHolder Interview call.

THOSE WHO PROVIDED WRITING RETREAT SPACE:
Peter Barnes, Tomales Bay Institute, Mesa Refuge • Martha Coventry • William Frost • Nina Rothschild Utne, Lily Springs Farm • Zoë and Graham François • Life Science Foundation Retreat Center • Oak Ridge Conference Center • Susan Kraus • Gary and Nanci Smaby • Will and Lynette Raap

INDEX

Italicized page numbers indicate illustrations.

S

T

U

V

W

ABOUT HEARTLAND

Staying Connected

HEARTLAND—THE CONVENING COMPANY

Heartland convenes conversations, programs, trainings, and communities of engagement to practice the skills of the intentional leader, dedicated to creating a world that works for all.

We offer authentic conversation, support, leadership development, and inspiration in every program and training.

Visit http://heartlandcircle.com/

THE CONVENING INSTITUTE

The Convening Institute represents the interests of all convening and Art of Convening activities. The purpose of the Institute is to further the vision and mission of convening in the world while providing learning, training, advocacy, and research capabilities via virtual and in-person communities of engagement.

The Art of Convening Trainings

The Art of Convening Trainings are offered in several forms. In all Trainings, the participants travel the inner and outer path of the Convener, from *The Heart of the Matter* to *Commitment to Action* and all the territory in-between. These immensely practical trainings elicit the best and brightest inherent in each participant, leading to transformed engagements and meetings that deliver responsibility, accountability, and commitment. Available to individuals and organizations.

Visit http://heartlandcircle.com/AoC-main.htm

The Graduate Guild

The purpose of the Guild is to support, and encourage AoC Training graduates in the continual experiential learning via the practice, experimentation, inquiry, discovery, growth, and mastery of many dimensions of the AoC.

Visit http://heartlandcircle.com/AoC-main.htm

THE THOUGHT LEADER GATHERINGS—A COMMUNITY OF ENGAGEMENT FOR LEADERS

These member-based, monthly morning "conversations," held in Minnesota and the San Francisco Bay Area, bring together leaders in corporate, nonprofit, and independent organizations who are devoted to combining visionary and on-the-ground discourse.

The TLGs are held in venues conducive to healthy human interaction. The format of each four-hour session is designed to stimulate and reveal the collective wisdom of the group in an efficient yet unhurried time frame. Drawing on ancient and modern group processes, the sessions open with remarks from a "conversation starter" and close with a "harvesting" session.

Visit http://heartlandcircle.com/tlg-main.htm

THE VISIONHOLDER INTERVIEWS

The Heartland VisionHolder Interviews feature prominent authors and thought leaders in a provocative interactive teleconference. Join us for an hour of generative conversation. Each call is free. Details are e-mailed when you register.

Visit http://heartlandcircle.com/vh-upcoming.htm

THE HEARTLAND NETWORK

The Heartland Network connects, convenes, and supports a Community of Evolutionary Leaders engaged in creating well-being for all in our communities, our organizations, and the world. Members are listed in our online directory and are part of an emerging new membership Network culture.

Through our online social media network site, both members and guests connect with and have access to a global network of thought leaders like themselves, bringing a new vision to a conversation that is creating a new world.

Visit http://heartlandcircle.com/hnm-learnmore.htm

THE MEN'S WILDERNESS JOURNEY

Twice yearly, Craig Neal leads eight men on a guided journey of inner reflection and discovery into America's most pristine wilderness. This is an opportunity to pause and take an intentional time-out to consider what is next. The beauty and wildness of the Boundary Waters Wilderness Canoe Area of northern Minnesota inspires all who take this journey.

Visit http://heartlandcircle.com/MWJ-main.htm

SUBSCRIBE TO OUR BLOG

http://heartlandcircle.blogs.com/circle/

BE IN TOUCH

We welcome being contacted at info@heartlandcircle.com or 612-920-3039.

ABOUT THE AUTHORS

Patricia Neal, Craig Neal, and Cynthia Wold

CRAIG NEAL

Since awakening to his life's purpose in 1963, Craig has celebrated life as a passionate evolutionary leader. He has been a publishing and organizational executive, as well as a guide to those called to authentically show up in life and work. Throughout the '70s, '80s, and '90s, Craig held executive positions with Garden Way, Inc., and Rodale Publishing, and helped launch *Harrowsmith* and *Eating Well* magazines. By 1996, he concluded his publishing career as publisher of *Utne Reader* magazine.

In 1996, Craig founded Heartland Inc. with Patricia, his wife of 30 years. Heartland produced the first Thought Leader Gathering in 1998. Twelve years and 170 Gatherings later, Craig has co-convened over 1,600 leaders from 800 organizations in these ongoing membership-based groups in Minnesota and the San Francisco Bay Area. He and Patricia created the Essential Conversations Process for educators (Circle of Fire) and MBA students, and have convened meetings for businesses and communities alike.

Craig created and launched the Art of Convening Trainings in 2004 for those called to be an inspired catalyst for change in their organization or community. Over 350 are currently engaged or have graduated from 40 groups.

Craig's passion for the wilderness and being among men transforming their lives and personal visions led him to create the Men's Wilderness Journeys.

Craig is skilled at building relationships within and across organizations. He is dedicated to creating networks of authenticity and essential conversations among individuals and within organizations through training and convening events.

He founded the Conscious Business Alliance and the Minnesota Magazine Publishers Association, and served as a board member of Business for Social Responsibility, various Waldorf Schools, and Responsible Minnesota Business.

Craig and Patricia live in Minneapolis; they have three inspired adult children and two grandsons.

PATRICIA NEAL

"My passion is to bring convening as an expression of intentional leadership and transformation. I love to convene leaders and communities of engagement dedicated to creating a world with well-being for all."

Patricia is cofounder and president of Heartland Inc.

Since 1998, Patricia and her husband, Craig Neal, have co-convened over 170 Thought Leader Gatherings serving leaders in Minnesota and the San Francisco Bay Area. Patricia codeveloped the Art of Convening Trainings with Craig. Patricia leads When Women Lead retreats for women leaders in Minnesota. Under Patricia's guidance and focus, Heartland's signature programs over the last decade-plus have flourished.

Prior to Heartland Inc., Patricia held various marketing and media positions at Telemedia Communications, where she helped launch two national magazines, *Harrowsmith* and *Eating Well*, and at Garden Way Mfg. Inc.

Patricia serves as a Founding Board member of Honoring Women Worldwide, and is a participant and advocate in the Waldorf School movement. She is mother to three outstanding grown children and grandmother to two terrific boys.

CYNTHIA WOLD

Cynthia believes that the loving and generous among us are heroes to be recognized.

She is a writer, artist, and Web marketer and designer. She started her own Web design and consulting business in 2000, helping high-value organizations and nonprofits to better communicate their value propositions, until joining the Heartland team in 2007 as its Web chief.

Cynthia raised her two daughters as a single parent, working as a bartender, restaurant manager, and teaching/research assistant while earning her B.A. in psychology, cum laude, Phi Beta Kappa, at the University of Minnesota.

She continues to serve in an advisory capacity for several nonprofit organizations, including Minnesota Alliance of Peacemakers.

Cynthia lives in Minneapolis with her husband, Tom, her two stepsons, her cat, and Polo the wonder dog.

Berrett-Koehler is an independent publisher dedicated to an ambitious mission: *Creating a World That Works for All.*

We believe that to truly create a better world, action is needed at all levels—individual, organizational, and societal. At the individual level, our publications help people align their lives with their values and with their aspirations for a better world. At the organizational level, our publications promote progressive leadership and management practices, socially responsible approaches to business, and humane and effective organizations. At the societal level, our publications advance social and economic justice, shared prosperity, sustainability, and new solutions to national and global issues.

A major theme of our publications is "Opening Up New Space." Berrett-Koehler titles challenge conventional thinking, introduce new ideas, and foster positive change. Their common quest is changing the underlying beliefs, mindsets, institutions, and structures that keep generating the same cycles of problems, no matter who our leaders are or what improvement programs we adopt.

We strive to practice what we preach—to operate our publishing company in line with the ideas in our books. At the core of our approach is stewardship, which we define as a deep sense of responsibility to administer the company for the benefit of all of our "stakeholder" groups: authors, customers, employees, investors, service providers, and the communities and environment around us.

We are grateful to the thousands of readers, authors, and other friends of the company who consider themselves to be part of the "BK Community." We hope that you, too, will join us in our mission.

A BK Business Book

This book is part of our BK Business series. BK Business titles pioneer new and progressive leadership and management practices in all types of public, private, and nonprofit organizations. They promote socially responsible approaches to business, innovative organizational change methods, and more humane and effective organizations.

A community dedicated to creating
a world that works for all

Visit Our Website: www.bkconnection.com

Read book excerpts, see author videos and Internet movies, read our authors' blogs, join discussion groups, download book apps, find out about the BK Affiliate Network, browse subject-area libraries of books, get special discounts, and more!

Subscribe to Our Free E-Newsletter, the *BK Communiqué*

Be the first to hear about new publications, special discount offers, exclusive articles, news about bestsellers, and more! Get on the list for our free e-newsletter by going to **www.bkconnection.com**.

Get Quantity Discounts

Berrett-Koehler books are available at quantity discounts for orders of ten or more copies. Please call us toll-free at (800) 929-2929 or email us at **bkp.orders@aidcvt.com**.

Join the BK Community

BKcommunity.com is a virtual meeting place where people from around the world can engage with kindred spirits to create a world that works for all. **BKcommunity.com** members may create their own profiles, blog, start and participate in forums and discussion groups, post photos and videos, answer surveys, announce and register for upcoming events, and chat with others online in real time. Please join the conversation!

Southern Methodist Univ
3 2177 02137 8011